Attainment's
Connections in the Workplace

Social Skills Reader

Written by June Stride, Ed.D.
Illustrated by Anthony Zammit

By June Stride, Ed. D.
Illustrated by Anthony Zammit
Edited by Tom Kinney, Rick Wolfsdorf and Rose Zammit
Graphic Design by Anthony Ribando and Maria Robertson

Attainment Company, Inc.

An Attainment/Wolfpack Publication
Printed in China.
© 2008 Attainment Company, Inc. All rights reserved.
ISBN: 1-57861-629-8

Attainment Company/ Wolfpack Multimedia Inc
P.O. Box 930160 Verona, Wisconsin
USA 53593-0160
1-800-327-4269
www.AttainmentCompany.com

Table of Contents

1 Fast Isn't Always Good 6
2 The New Bike 12
3 Talking It Over 18
4 Maria Prepares a Surprise 24
5 Maria's Decision 30
6 Maria's Bus Adventure 36
7 A Tough Decision 42
8 Not the Newest Anymore 48
9 The New Boy 54
10 All Locked Up 60
11 Just In Case 66
12 The Dream Job 72
13 An Attitude 78

Table of Contents

14	Jerome and the Surprise Package	84
15	The Golden Treasure	90
16	Misplaced Focus	96
17	The Good and the Bad	102
18	Lunchtime Crisis	108
19	Room for Improvement	114
20	Help! Papers Everywhere	120
21	Unexpected Changes	126
22	Did I Get That Right?	132
23	Sharing an Adventure	138
24	Good Stuff	144

25	The Invitation	150
26	Looking Good	156
27	The Dream	162
28	An Unkind Remark	168
29	The THINK Test	174
30	Doing the RSVP Thing	180
31	The Missing Employee	186
32	Broken Trust	192
33	Lighten Up	198
34	Keep Trying	204
35	Getting Ready	210

Vocabulary

plaid - *checkered appearance*
   Maria found her plaid slacks in the pile of clothes.

present - *introduce or put forward*
   How you present yourself when you have a job is important.

appropriate - *proper, correct*
   Check in the mirror to see if your clothes are appropriate for work.

inappropriate - *not proper, not correct*
   Dirty and mismatched clothes are inappropriate for work.

frustrated - *discouraged, feeling unsatisfied*
   Maria felt frustrated that she was not ready for breakfast.

novella

1 Fast Isn't Always Good!
Maria Gets Ready For Work

Maria hated to get up for work.

Maria hated to get up on workdays. Each morning, she turned off the alarm clock as soon as it rang. She liked to stay in bed and listen to the morning songbirds. She enjoyed the sounds of her family getting ready to start the day. As Maria turned over in bed to delay getting up, she heard her mother's footsteps in the hall.

Maria thought, "Good thing Mom didn't open the door all the way!"

A moment later, Maria heard her squeaky bedroom door open. Maria thought, "Good thing the lights are out so Mom can't see this room!"

"Time to get up and dress for work, Maria," her mother called. Maria stretched and got up. She pulled off her nightgown and threw it onto the pile of clothes on the floor. She poked her foot through those clothes looking for something to wear to work. She located the plaid slacks from Tuesday, her favorite Hawaiian shirt from Wednesday and yesterday's underwear and socks.

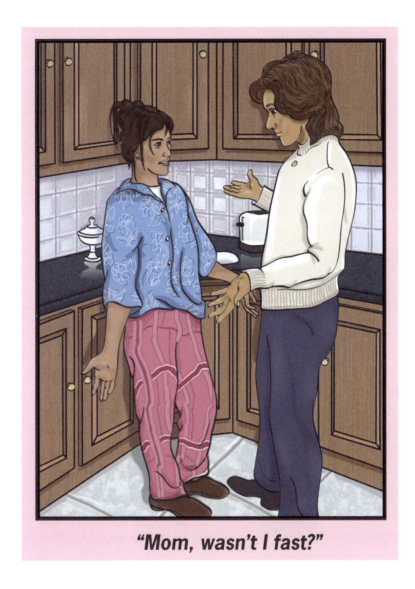

"Mom, wasn't I fast?"

Smiling, she pulled them on. Pleased she had dressed so quickly, Maria ran to the kitchen for breakfast. "Mom, wasn't I fast?" Maria asked excitedly.

Looking Maria over carefully, her Mom replied, "Well, Maria, fast is not always good. How you present yourself when you have a job is important. It means you need to think about how you look and dress."

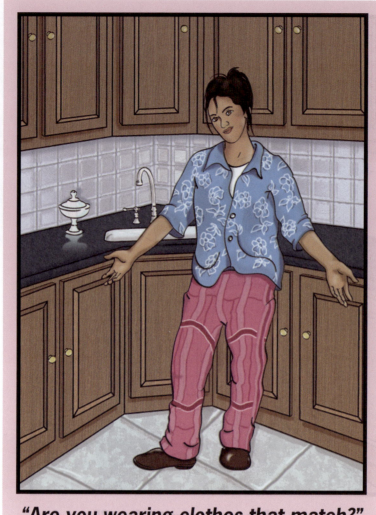

"Are you wearing clothes that match?"

Mom continued, "Did you take a shower? Are you wearing neat and clean clothes that match? Did you check in the mirror to see if you look appropriate for work? If not, no breakfast until you do!"

"Darn, Mom! How do you always know?"

Questions:

The look on Maria's face and her body language showed that Maria was:

        a. laughing   b. happy   c. frustrated

Sometimes people get upset and _____ when things don't turn out as they planned.

1. At what time of day does this story take place?
2. What was Maria expected to do?
3. What did Maria do that her mom did not agree with?
4. How could Maria have saved time so that fast would have been good?

Vocabulary

admiring - *pleased, appreciative*
Jerome was admiring the shiny, red convertible when the owner came up behind him.

elderly - *old, mature*
An elderly man joked with Jerome.

slacker - *lazy bones, loafer*
Jerome did not want to be a slacker on the job.

coworker - *person with whom you work*
Ellie was Jerome's coworker.

startled - *to be frightened*
Mrs. Green startled Jerome when she came up behind him.

novella 2

The New Bike
Working and Saving

"How do you like my new car, Jerome?"

Jerome was admiring a shiny red convertible in the BIG-BUY parking lot when the owner of the car came up behind him and startled him. "Hi, Jerome! How do you like my new car?"

"Oh boy," Jerome answered. "It's a beauty Mrs. Green. If I weren't working, I'd show you my new bike. It's red, too. I've been saving for it for a long time."

Jerome pushed the carts.

"Aren't we both lucky?" Jerome continued, "Last week I had enough to buy the bike and a helmet. Mom says no riding the bike unless I wear the helmet. Gotta go now. Have a nice day, Mrs. Green."

Smiling widely, Jerome walked over to the next shopping cart and pushed it into the shopping cart return space. He saw several more carts scattered throughout the parking lot and headed off to bring them back to the return space. With a little struggle, he was able to get each inside the other to make a long train. Looking around to be sure there were no cars or people in the way, he pushed them up to the front of the supermarket. He neatly arranged them up against the wall so that customers could easily grab one on the way in to shop.

Jerome admired his polished red bike in the rack.

Before heading toward the double entry doors, he took one admiring look at his new, polished, red bike in the bike rack. Jerome was on his way into BIG-BUY when one of his favorite customer friends called over to him, "Hey, Jerome, what's happening? You hanging around doing nothing?" the elderly man asked, laughing.

"Hi, Mr. Kelly. No, I've been working." Jerome knew Mr. Kelly liked to tease him so Jerome didn't get upset. Jerome did not like people to think he was a slacker. He wanted his boss and his job coach to know that he took his job seriously, even if he did chat with the customers.

"Do you want paper or plastic bags?"

Jerome continued into the store. He went directly to the checkout counter where his favorite coworker, Ellie, worked the register. He got started right away. He separated the food items that Ellie pushed down to his end of the counter. He looked up to the young lady customer and smiled to greet her. Jerome continued, "Hello. Do you want plastic bags or paper bags?" Separating the frozen foods from the vegetables as he bagged, Jerome carefully placed the groceries in her cart.

As he looked up, he noticed Shana, his job coach, pass through the double doors. Jerome's face lit up. Turning to Ellie, he said, "She came! I hoped she would. I want to show her my new bike that I paid for all by myself."

Questions:

Jerome's face lit up when he saw Shana. His expression showed that he felt:
        a. annoyed   b. depressed   c. delighted

When we see someone that we like very much, our facial expression may show that we feel _____.

    1. What did Mrs. Green and Jerome have in common?

    2. For what reason was Jerome so pleased?

    3. How might things have been different if Jerome did not work at BIG-BUY?

    4. What behaviors showed that Jerome wanted to be a good employee?

The New Bike | Page 17

Vocabulary

application - *form used to request (a job)*
Shana helped Jerome correctly fill out an application to work at BIG-BUY.

responsibilities - *tasks, everyday jobs*
Shana discussed the job responsibilities with Jerome.

interview - *talk with someone, to share special information*
Jerome had a job interview with Mr. Daniels.

habit - *routine, practiced behavior*
Jerome had gotten into the habit of drinking juice instead of soda.

anxious - *concerned, worried, nervous*
Shana was anxious to see Jerome's new bike.

novella

3 Talking It Over
The Job Coach Helps Out

"I'm so glad that you came to see me."

Jerome looked at his watch. It was 12:00 sharp. Just as Jerome began walking towards the employee lounge for his lunch break, he saw Shana wheel her way though the double doors of BIG-BUY.

Jerome called excitedly, "Shana! I'm so glad that you came today. I can't wait to show you my new red bike!"

Jerome always looked forward to seeing Shana. He would never forget that it was Shana who had helped him get his job at BIG-BUY.

"I'll be right back."

Shana had helped him with his application, explained about the job responsibilities and helped prepare him for the job interview with Mr. Daniels. She even celebrated with him after he had been hired. Now that he was a BIG-BUY employee, she stopped by a few times a week to see how everything was going.

Smiling at Jerome, Shana said, "Hi, Jerome. I'm just going to check with Mr. Daniels that it's okay for us to eat lunch together in the lounge. I'll be right back." With that, Shana wheeled herself briskly over to the manager's office.

He wanted his carts neat and clean.

While Jerome was waiting for Shana, he noticed that there were no customers waiting on Ellie's line. He also noticed that some of the shopping carts had trash in them. He wanted his carts to be clean and neat. Since there were no customers, he went over and emptied the carts of the old newspaper fliers. He straightened up the little blue canvas tote baskets. Standing back he thought, "Now they look ready for our shoppers."

"We're all set, Jerome," Shana called. "Let's treat ourselves to a bottle of juice while we chat." Jerome had noticed that Shana never drank soda. She always bought a bottle of juice instead and Jerome had gotten into that habit, too. Juice in hand, they headed for the employee lounge.

Shana had so many questions.

Shana plunked her juice bottle down as she moved her wheelchair next to the chairs surrounding the table. "Jerome, I'm anxious to hear all about that new red bike. Do you ride it to work everyday? What route do you take? Do you have a good lock for it? Do you wear a helmet? Also, how about your paychecks now? What are you doing with the money? Perhaps we should talk about a bank account for you."

"Gee, Shana, you always have so much to say." Jerome sighed. "You always have so many questions, too. After we talk, I want to show you my new bike. Then, will you show me how your van lifts you and your wheelchair?"

Questions:

The look on Shana's face and her body language showed that Shana was:
      a. pleased   b. angry   c. frustrated

Employees who demonstrate good work habits make their employers feel _____ .

    1. Why did Jerome especially want to see Shana?
    2. Name three ways that Jerome's job coach helped him.
    3. How might Jerome's life be different without Shana's help?
    4. Tell two ways Shana is helping Jerome be a better employee.

Vocabulary

supposed to - *expected, take for granted*
Maria knew she was supposed to eat breakfast before leaving for work.

relax - *unwind, calm down*
Maria's mother told her to relax and think about what she needed to do.

grateful - *thankful*
Maria was sure that her mother would be grateful for the surprise breakfast.

obvious - *clear, plain to see*
It was obvious that Maria's mother felt rotten.

insisted - *stated something firmly*
Mother always insisted on breakfast before work.

puzzled - *confused about something*
Maria felt puzzled about how to make breakfast.

novella

4 Maria Prepares A Surprise
Breakfast Before Work

Mom must feel rotten.

Maria felt sad when she saw her mom still in bed. It was obvious she felt rotten. Mom never stayed in bed. She always insisted on making breakfast for Maria on workdays.

Maria was hungry. She knew she was supposed to eat before going to work. She also wanted to do something nice for her mom. She thought, "I'll make a surprise breakfast!"

Maria Prepares A Surprise | Page 25

First I have to wash and dry.

Maria looked around the kitchen, puzzled about what to do. She knew the first thing was to wash and dry her hands. Then she remembered Mom saying, "Relax, Maria. Think about what you need in order to do a job."

Maria decided that she would get all of the breakfast stuff.

Maria decided that she would get all the breakfast 'stuff' and put it on the counter. She opened cupboard doors until she found the toaster. She placed it on the counter. But toast is no fun without peanut butter and jelly. She got the peanut butter and grape jelly from the refrigerator. She placed a knife and spoon next to the peanut butter and the jelly. "I need plates and paper napkins, too," she thought.

Then, she put two pieces of bread in the toaster and pushed down the toaster lever. A minute later, POP! Up came two lovely, golden pieces of toast.

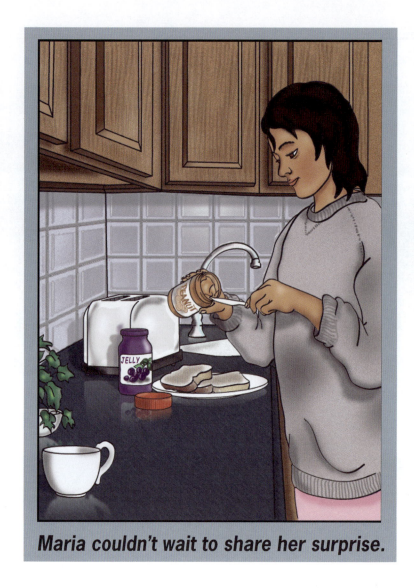

Maria couldn't wait to share her surprise.

She took the knife and spread the peanut butter onto the toast. Then she unscrewed the top of the jelly jar and put a spoonful of jelly on each piece. Next, she got two glasses and poured the orange juice. Maria felt proud. She thought, "Mom will really be grateful that I am helping out. Now she can get the rest she needs and still eat breakfast."

Maria gently pushed her mom's bedroom door open with her foot as she carefully held the breakfast tray. With a proud grin, she announced, "Surprise, Mom! I made you breakfast and I did it all by myself! Now, you and I can eat together before I have to leave for work."

Questions:

The look on Maria's mother's face and her body language showed that she was:
        a. angry   b. grateful   c. crying

When we show kindness to others, they are _____ because we show them how much we care.

    1. How did Maria know that her mother was not feeling well?

    2. What did Maria decide to do?

    3. How do you think Maria's mom felt about Maria's breakfast choices? Why?

    4. How is eating breakfast related to work behavior?

Vocabulary

protect - *guard, save from*
    Maria needed to protect her clothes from the rain.

identification card - *card that gives information that allows another to recognize you*
    Maria took her identification card with her whenever she went out.

prompt card - *a listing of tips to help do or remember something*
    Maria often used a prompt card when she was unsure how to do something.

blazer - *sport jacket*
    Maria decided that the blazer would not be good to wear.

poncho - *waterproof garment with a hood, worn over clothing*
    Maria slipped the poncho on to protect her clothing from the rain.

novella

5 Maria's Decision

Weather and Work

She could hear the rain and wind beating against her window.

Maria looked out the window. She could hear the wind pushing the rain against the window. She looked around the yard. She thought, "The wind is bending branches of the trees. The rain has made large puddles in the walkway."

She opened the closet door and looked for something to wear.

"I need to wear something to protect my good work clothes," she decided. She opened the closet door and looked for a coat to wear. Which one? Should she wear the short blazer jacket or maybe the heavy wool jacket? No, it was not cold. It was windy and rainy. Those jackets would not keep her dry. The TV weatherman had said rainy and windy all day. She spotted her blue poncho and umbrella.

"Hmm…," she thought, "I think my raincoat and a scarf would be good for this weather." She took her raincoat and slipped into it. In the pocket, she found a matching scarf.

Let me check that all the stuff I need is here.

Maria looked down at her watch. It was 7:10. She had to catch the bus in 20 minutes. She couldn't miss the bus or she would be late for work. Now where was her backpack? She found it on the table next to the closet. She opened it to check that all of the stuff she needed was in there. Maria took each item out of her backpack and laid it on the table.

"Let's see," Maria thought, "I have my prompt card, my bus pass, my comb, my wallet, my house keys and my pen. Yes... that's it. I've got everything and I even remembered to double check just like mom always tells me!"

Feeling pleased, Maria carefully placed each item into the backpack again and headed for the front door.

Maria's Decision

The rain made puddles on the stairs.

Maria called good-bye to her mom. As she opened the front door she felt the raindrops tapping on her hands. "Wow," Maria thought. "It's a good thing I'm prepared!"

Maria quickly opened the umbrella over her head. Carefully, she went down the steps. Avoiding puddles, Maria made her way along the sidewalk, thinking, "I'm right on time to catch the bus for work."

Questions:

The look on Maria's face and her body language showed that Maria was:
     a. angry   b. sad   c. thinking

Sometimes people show they are _____ by putting their hand up to their chin while they consider the best choice.

1. What kind of weather did Maria see as she looked out of her window?
2. In what way did the weather affect Maria's choice of clothing?
3. What might have happened if Maria left for the bus without checking the contents of her backpack?
4. How could Maria's decisions about rain gear relate to her job?

Maria's Decision | Page 35

Vocabulary

independent - *self-sufficient, able to do something on one's own*
Maria enjoyed being independent enough to travel on the public bus.

stranger - *unfamiliar person, someone not known*
Maria did not talk to the stranger reading the newspaper.

decision - *choice*
She made a decision to sit up front behind the bus driver.

fare - *fee, charge*
Everyone put the fare in the machine after boarding the bus.

required - *necessary*
A sign reminded people that the exact fare was required.

reduced - *made less*
Some passengers used a reduced fare pass.

novella

6 Maria's Bus Adventure
Independent Travel To Work

"No, I'm not taking time to pet Sam."

The bus stop was two blocks from Maria's house. It took her 10 minutes to get there if she did not waste time. She walked quickly, not stopping to pat Sam, the neighbor's new puppy. She mumbled to herself, "No, I'm not taking time to pat Sam."

She smiled and said hello to the people she knew.

When she arrived at the bus stop, she took a seat under the shelter and looked around. Some of her friends from the neighborhood were there waiting for the bus to take them to work, too. She smiled and said hello to the people she knew. She wondered if the man reading the paper was a 'stranger' she shouldn't talk to. Luckily, he was reading the paper so she didn't have to make a decision.

Maria was glad she was a few minutes early so she could check her prompt card for taking the bus. She looked at it carefully. It said, "Bus Number N19, exact fare required." The fare was one dollar with her reduced fare bus pass. Just as she took out her money and her pass, bus N19 pulled up. Maria put her backpack on and stood up to wait on line to board.

She showed her pass and put a dollar's worth of change in the machine.

It didn't take long for everyone to board the bus. In fact, it seemed like only a minute had passed before it was Maria's turn to board. She climbed the bus steps, happy to see the welcome smile of Jack, the usual bus driver. She returned his smile while glancing at the sign on the fare box. Then she showed her pass and put a dollar's worth of change in the machine. She asked Jack to remind her when the bus got to Center Street so she could get off. She took the seat in the front nearest to Jack to make sure she was able to hear his reminder.

She waved good-bye to Jack.

Maria enjoyed the bus ride to work. She watched school children come from their homes and begin the walk to school. She saw parents back cars out of driveways and dogs watch sadly through windows as family members left for the day. She felt a part of the world as she sat with others on the bus heading to work.

Before long, the bus driver called out "Center Street." Maria stood up and carefully checked that she had all of her belongings. Calling good-bye to Jack, she got off the bus as soon as it came to a complete stop. Grinning at her success, she walked the short distance to work.

Questions:

The look on Maria's face and her body language showed that she was:
    a. angry   b. proud   c. crying

When we are successful meeting a challenge, we usually feel _____.

1. How long did it take Maria to walk to the bus stop?
2. What are two things that Maria did that helped her have a safe bus trip to work?
3. How might Maria's day have been changed if she had forgotten her prompt card?
4. Why is it important to get to work on time?

Maria's Bus Adventure | Page 41

Vocabulary

ignored - *unnoticed, unseen*
Some of the employees ignored Jerome.

clustered - *grouped or collected around*
The guys always clustered around James.

decision - *choice*
Jerome had a hard time making a decision about loaning his bike.

barely - *only, just about*
Jerome barely had time to think before James took the key.

especially - *in most cases, singled out for something*
James was especially friendly to Jerome when he wanted to use the bike.

particularly - *more than usual, to a great extent*
Jerome wondered about friends, particularly about James.

novella

7 A Tough Decision
Making Friends On The Job

At other times, James treated Jerome like he didn't exist.

Jerome wanted people to like him, especially the high school employees at BIG-BUY. Some of the grown ups were really friendly. A few of the high school kids were. But some of the guys ignored him. Once in a while, he heard them laughing when he walked by. He wondered why.

Jerome wondered particularly about James. The other guys always clustered around James. He seemed to have lots of friends. At times, James went out of his way to talk to Jerome. At other times, he acted as if Jerome didn't exist.

A Tough Decision | Page 43

Since Jerome had his new bike, James seemed more interested in Jerome.

Since Jerome had his new bike, James seemed more interested in Jerome. In fact, when he went out to look at Jerome's bike, he said, "That bike is a beauty. It needs a name. 'Big Red', that's what I'll call it. I wish I had one like it."

That made Jerome feel good. Maybe James was beginning to be a friend. That's why it was such a tough decision when James asked Jerome if he could borrow 'Big Red' sometime. Jerome wanted to say no but he was afraid James wouldn't like him so he said yes.

"I'll be careful with 'Big Red'."

"Jerome, okay if I take 'Big Red' to Burger Mac today?" James asked. "I'll be careful with 'Big Red'. No need for you to worry about that."

Jerome barely had time to think before James continued, "Hey, isn't this the key to the lock here in your pocket?" James did not wait for Jerome to reply. Laughing, he put his hand into Jerome's shirt pocket, grabbed the key to the bicycle lock and zipped out the door.

He was not happy that James was always taking 'Big Red'.

From that day on, James continually seemed to need 'Big Red' for some special reason. Jerome noticed that James was super friendly around lunchtime before he took 'Big Red'. When James returned with 'Big Red', he rarely thanked Jerome. During the rest of the day, James paid little attention to him.

Jerome thought that James' behavior was strange. He wished James would save money and buy his own bike. He was not happy that James was always taking 'Big Red', but Jerome was unsure what to do about it. He thought, "Maybe Shana can help me figure out what to do."

Questions:

Jerome's face showed how he felt about James taking 'Big Red'. He felt:
        a. unhappy   b. surprised   c. joyful

When people take advantage of us and our belongings, they sometimes make us feel _____ .

1. What name did James give Jerome's bike?

2. Tell two things that James did that made Jerome wonder if he was a friend.

3. What do you think would have happened if Jerome told James he could not use his bike?

4. Why is it important to have friends at work?

A Tough Decision | Page 47

Vocabulary

amazingly - *surprisingly*
Amazingly, anger left Maria when she saw the frightened and nervous look on the new boy's face.

routines - *habits*
Maria was learning the new routines required at work.

disturb - *interrupt, upset*
Maria did not want to disturb Shana's work.

interrupt - *bother, interfere*
Maria did not want to interrupt Shana during an important phone call.

rude - *disagreeable, not polite*
Maria turned to call the new boy a rude dummy.

novella

8 Not The Newest Anymore
Social Behavior At Work

The new boy bumped into her.

Maria walked up to the counter in the front office and carefully wrote her name on the line next to her name on the sign-in sheet. Then she walked over to the time clock and took her card from the rack of punch cards. She was about to punch in when a new boy bumped into her and made her drop her card.

Not The Newest Anymore | Page 49

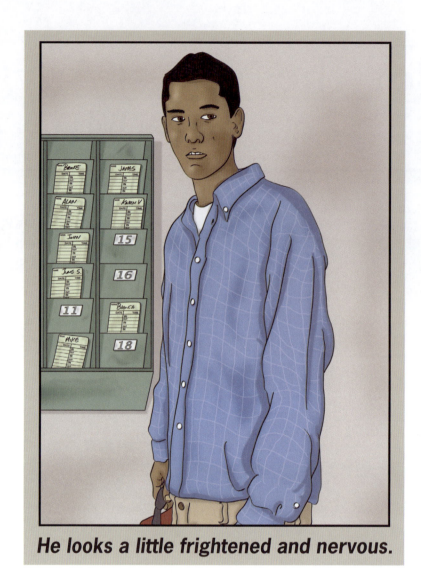
He looks a little frightened and nervous.

    Maria turned to call him a 'rude dummy'. She looked up at the new boy's face. She thought, "Gosh, he looks a little frightened and nervous." She recalled her job coach telling her to think before she said anything that might hurt someone's feelings. Amazingly, her anger left her. She remembered how scared she had been when she started working three months ago. Surprising herself, she said "Hi" to the new boy and showed him where to put his card in the rack.

The clock on the wall said 7:56.

Maria felt proud. She was no longer the 'new girl'. She was learning the routines at work. She was learning how to hold her temper. She could even help someone else who didn't know what to do yet. She knew there still was a lot to learn, but somehow she would.

Maria walked back to her workstation and put her backpack in her locker. She noticed the clock on the wall. It was 7:56. She had four minutes before she was to meet with Shana, her job coach. Just last week, Shana had told Maria how important it was to report on time ready for work. Maria wanted to prove she could be responsible. Maria longed to stop and talk to her friends, but she didn't. She went directly to Shana to tell her she was ready to begin work.

It was more polite to wait for Shana.

Maria stopped outside of the door of Shana's office. She stood quietly watching Shana check through some papers on her desk. She did not want to disturb Shana's work. Last week Maria had burst into the room to greet Shana and had interrupted Shana in an important phone call. Shana had not been angry. She had explained that it was more polite for Maria to wait until she had finished what she was doing before expecting her to talk with Maria.

Questions:

The look on Alan's face showed that he was:
        a. happy   b. excited   c. concerned

When people are in new situations and they feel unsure, their faces and body language may show that they are _____.

    1. What was the new boy's name?

    2. Why did Maria want to call him a 'rude dummy'? Why didn't she do it?

    3. What might have happened if Maria did call the new boy a 'rude dummy'?

    4. What are two ways that Maria demonstrated good work skills?

Not The Newest Anymore | Page 53

Vocabulary

relieved - *thankful, comforted*
Maria was relieved that the new boy seemed to know what to say.

introductions - *presenting yourself or something of interest to others*
Maria forgot all about the lesson on introductions.

extended - *reached out*
Maria extended her hand to the new boy.

decision - *choice*
Maria made a quick decision to help the new boy with his locker.

manage - *to be able to do something, to handle something*
The new boy could not manage to open his locker.

novella

9 The New Boy
Helping Others At Work

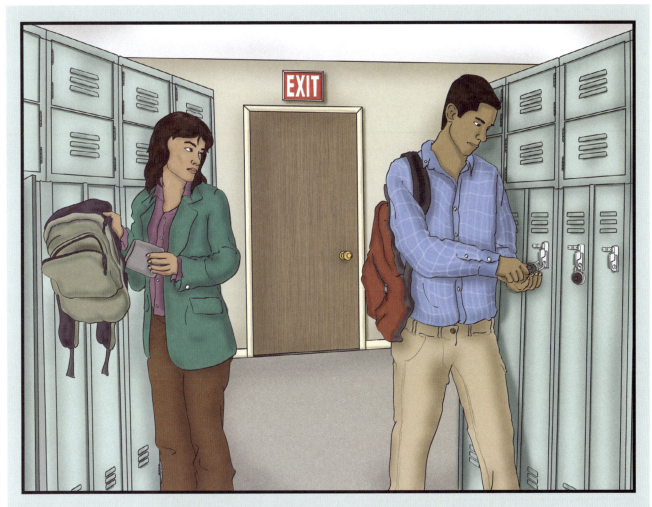

"He is cute, but he sure needs help."

Maria was ready to go for her break. As she opened her locker to get money from her backpack, she noticed the new boy trying to open his locker.

"Hmm," she thought. "He's kind of cute but he sure needs help. First he doesn't know where to put his time card, now he can't manage his locker."

The New Boy | Page 55

He grinned and Maria turned red.

Should she try to help him? Maria was torn. It was her morning break time. She had only 20 minutes to eat a snack. She was hungry. No one had helped her when she was new. Besides, she didn't even know his name. Grabbing her money, she turned to walk away. At the same moment, the new boy also turned. Smack, they bumped straight into each other.

He grinned.

Maria turned red. Gosh, he was tall! And he was cuter looking than she recalled. "What's wrong with me? I feel like my mind has gone blank," she thought.

"This is my first day at work."

Maria forgot everything about how to introduce herself. She was at a loss for words.

The new boy did not seem to be. Looking straight into Maria's eyes, he said, "Hi, I'm Alan Stanley. I'm new here. This is my first day at work. I guess you figured that out."

Maria felt relieved that the new boy seemed to know what to say. As he talked, the lesson on introductions flooded back into her head.

"Could you help me open my locker?"

Maria looked directly at the new boy and extended her hand. "Hi, Alan Stanley, new boy. I am Maria. I used to be the new girl here! Now that you are here, I am no longer the newest employee!"

Alan did not seem shy. He seemed to like to talk. He said, "Maria, I am having some problems today. You helped me with my time card. Could you help me open my locker?"

Maria made a quick decision to help. Maybe she could even wait until lunch to eat.

Page 58 | Chapter 9

Questions:

Maria and Alan bumped into each other. Maria's face showed that she was:
        a. tired   b. surprised   c. sad

When we accidentally bump into someone that we like, our faces and body language show we are _____ and embarrassed.

1. What problem did the new boy have?

2. What was the new boy's name?

3. Maria and the new boy had different talents. What could Maria do that the new boy could not? What was the new boy able to do that Maria could not do?

4. How might have things been different if Maria had not helped the new boy?

The New Boy | Page 59

Vocabulary

approached - *come close*
Maria had mixed feelings as 5 o'clock approached.

remote control - *almost automatically*
Maria was operating on remote control as she headed down to her locker.

immediately - *at once, right now*
Maria's face turned immediately to a smile when she saw the new boy.

combination - *arrangement of numbers to open a lock*
Maria said that she was pretty good with combination locks.

entrance - *doorway or opening*
The entrance doors will not be locked.

novella
10 All Locked Up
Offering Help

"Hi, Maria!"

As 5 o'clock approached, Maria noticed her mixed feelings. She wanted to stay at work but yet she wanted to go. In truth, she was really operating on 'remote control' as she headed down to her locker to get her backpack. A cheerful "Hi, Maria!" startled her. She noticed it was the new boy. Her face turned immediately to a smile when she saw him.

All Locked Up | Page 61

"I am worried that I might not be able to go home."

"Hello, Alan Stanley, 'new boy', how did it go on your first day? Do you think you will like working here?" Maria asked in a joyful voice.

"Well, I think so. I like the people. The job part seems confusing, though. I have so much to learn. Right now, I am worried that I might not be able to go home," Alan responded.

Puzzled, Maria asked, "What do you mean that you are afraid you might not be able to go home? No one will lock you up in here! You only need to punch out, open the entrance doors and head home."

"Maybe I can help."

"Yes, I know that sounds easy, especially to you. I'm not worried about being locked up in here; it's my stuff in my locker that I'm worried about. It's locked up in this locker and as many times as I try, I can't seem to get it open."

"Hmm," Maria answered, "maybe I can help."

"Gosh, I'd like that!" Alan replied.

All Locked Up | Page 63

"Would you like me to try and open it for you?"

Maria said, "I'm pretty good with combination locks. Would you like me to try to open it for you? I'll need that paper with the combination on it, please."

"Thanks, Maria. You saved me twice today. You are just like my personal lifeguard," Alan replied with a laugh.

"No problem, Alan. I bet you will soon be able to manage that locker," Maria quietly answered back. Using the combination, Maria easily opened the locker. With a grin, she turned to Alan. "Now let me help you do it!"

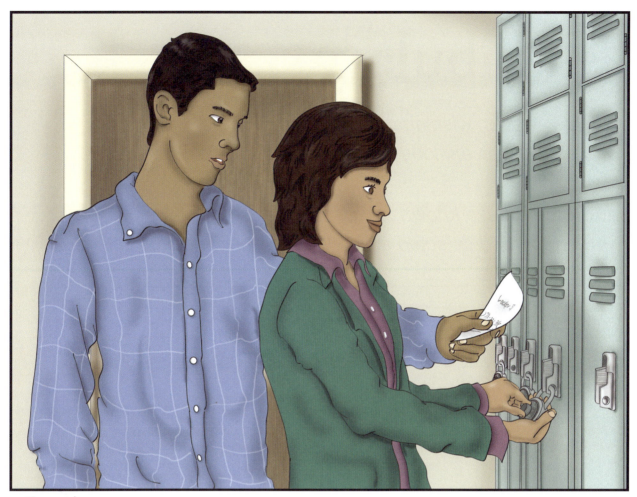

Questions:

Maria helped Alan open his locker. The look on Maria's face showed that she was:

      a. pleased   b. sad   c. angry

When we can help friends solve problems, we feel _____ with ourselves.

1. Who did Maria meet at her locker?
2. What worry did the 'new boy' have?
3. How do you think Maria's actions helped the 'new boy' feel more comfortable about work?
4. Find the sentences in which Maria accepts thanks and encourages the 'new boy' about opening his locker.

All Locked Up | Page 65

Vocabulary

anxious - *eager, wishing very much*
    Jerome was anxious to hear his cell phone ring.

announce - *make known*
    Jerome had selected a little tune to announce his cell phone calls.

incoming - *received*
    Jerome waited for an incoming call on his cell phone.

disappointed - *let down*
    Disappointed, Jerome re-clipped the phone to his belt.

novella
11 Just in Case

Phony Friends

"Ellie, look what my mom got me for my birthday."

Jerome proudly clipped his brand new cell phone to his belt. He was anxious to hear the little tune that he had selected to announce an incoming call.

After punching his time card at BIG-BUY, Jerome headed over to Ellie's check out counter. "Ellie, look what my mom got me for my birthday!" Jerome said.

On his break, he showed the guys his new phone.

"She said that now that I have a regular job and travel to work on my own, I should have a cell phone. Just in case she said. But just in case of what?" Jerome questioned.

Ellie said smiling, "Terrific, Jerome! It should come in very handy, just in case…"

All morning, Jerome had his new cell phone on his mind. On his break, he showed the guys his new phone.

"What's your number 'J'?" one of the guys asked.

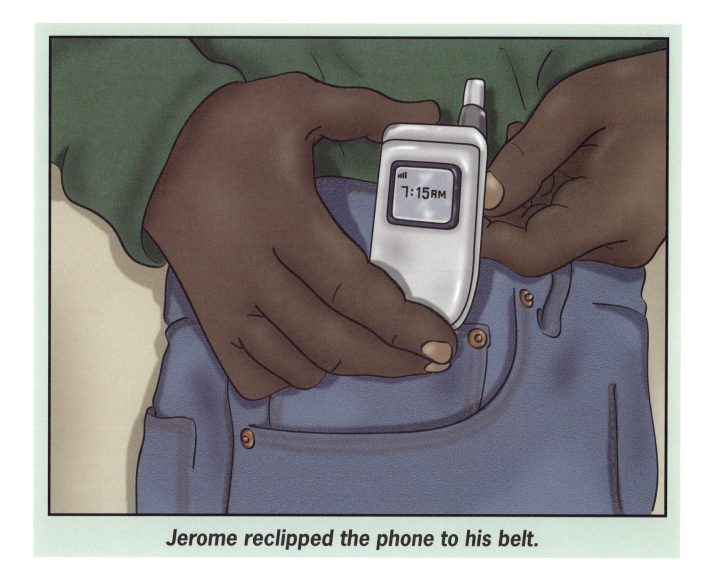

Jerome reclipped the phone to his belt.

As Jerome told his number, he thought about being called 'J'. Smiling, he thought, "Hmm… two new things today: a new cell phone and a nickname. I never had either before."

Not long after his break, Jerome heard 'the tune'. He quickly pulled the phone off of his belt and answered "Hello." There was no reply. Disappointed, Jerome reclipped the phone to his belt. A few minutes later, 'the tune' announced another call. Excitedly, Jerome got his cell and pushed the button. He loudly said, "Hello." Again there was no reply. Two more times 'the tune' played. Jerome answered and both times no one responded.

Just in Case | Page 69

"If you were wondering who made those calls, look who is coming."

"Ellie," he asked, "why would someone call me and then hang up when I answer?"

Ellie turned to Jerome and said, "Jerome, remember how your parents said 'just in case'? Well, just in case you were wondering who made those phone calls, look who is coming."

At that moment, James walked by Jerome with a grin on his face, "Hey 'J', anything happening with that new cell phone?"

Questions:

Someone called Jerome and hung up. The look on Jerome's face showed he was:

        a. confused   b. bored   c. happy

When people play tricks on us, they make us feel _____.

1. What did Jerome get for his birthday?
2. Why did Jerome feel frustrated about the phone calls?
3. What might have happened if Jerome had not given out his phone number?
4. How could a cell phone be helpful to an employee like Jerome?

Just in Case | Page 71

Vocabulary

employee - *worker*
    Sara was one of the best cafeteria employees.

cafeteria - *dining hall*
    Maria wanted to work in the cafeteria.

continued - *nonstop, constant*
    Shana continued to explain about the training program.

trainee - *learner, beginner*
    Shana explained that not all trainees, who want the cafeteria job, are able to do all that is expected.

tasks - *jobs*
    Sara had many tasks that she needed to do.

annoyed - *mildly angry, upset*
    Maria was annoyed that Shana assigned her to watch instead of work.

novella
12 The Dream Job
Training For A New Job

Thrilled, Maria hurried to report to Shana.

Shana, Maria's job coach, had already trained Maria to file papers. Maria thought filing was a fun job but working in the employee's cafeteria was Maria's dream.

Today Shana had promised to start training Maria for cafeteria work. Thrilled, Maria hurried to report in to Shana. Excitedly, she told Shana what fun cafeteria work would be.

The Dream Job | Page 73

"It won't be hard for me. I love to talk to people and I love to eat!"

Shana startled Maria by announcing that cafeteria work was difficult.

Maria interrupted Shana and said, "It won't be hard for me. I know I will be a good worker. I love to talk to people and I love to eat!"

Shana smiled and continued, "Not all trainees who want the job are able to do what is expected. Training can take several weeks. Today you will begin the first part of training by watching Sara work. She is one of our best cafeteria employees. Watch carefully to see what she does and what she doesn't do. First, count to see how many different tasks Sara does. Second, see when Sara talks and how often she talks. Later, we will discuss what you have seen.

She filled each glass with ice water.

At first, Maria was annoyed. She wanted to work, not watch Sara work. Before long, employees started coming in for a snack at break-time. Maria's interest increased. She was surprised that Sara smiled at everyone but did not talk to anyone. As soon as people were seated, Sara turned the glasses right side up on the table. Then she got a pitcher of iced water and filled each glass.

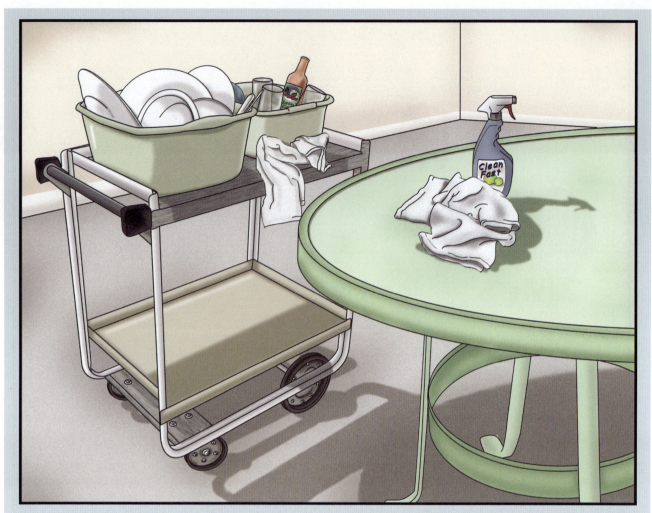

She made certain that the table was clean and dry before resetting it.

People thanked Sara.

Sara smiled and said, "You're welcome," but nothing else.

After people left, Sara took dirty glasses and flatware and put them in a bin. She took a spray bottle and carefully sprayed and wiped the table with paper towels. She made certain that the table was clean and dry before resetting it. Then, Sara stood back and waited for the next customers.

Questions:

Shana told Maria that the cafeteria job was difficult. Maria's hand to her chin showed that she was:

        a. happy   b. sad   c. thinking

What people do with their hands sometimes show us what they are _____.

1. What was Maria's 'dream job'?
2. Why did Maria feel that the dream job would be easy for her?
3. What might have happened if Shana had let Maria work on the first training day?
4. Why do you think Shana felt that watching Sara work would help Maria learn about her dream job?

The Dream Job | Page 77

Vocabulary

performed - *done, carried out*
 Maria remembered the tasks that Sara had performed.

physical - *having to do with the body*
 Maria was able to list all the physical duties.

eye contact - *look directly into someone's eyes*
 Sara always made eye contact and said hello to customers.

blurted - *exclaimed, cried out*
 Maria blurted out, "I don't think she was social."

groomed - *neat, cleaned up*
 Sara made a well groomed appearance as a cafeteria worker.

novella

13 An Attitude
Training For A New Job

Think about Sara's social responsibility.

Shana took Maria to her office to talk about Maria's first cafeteria training session. Together, they made a chart of the different tasks that Sara had done.

Shana said, "Maria, it's great that you remembered the tasks and even the order in which Sara performed them. You were able to list her physical duties. Now think about what Sara did that was part of her social responsibility."

An Attitude | Page 79

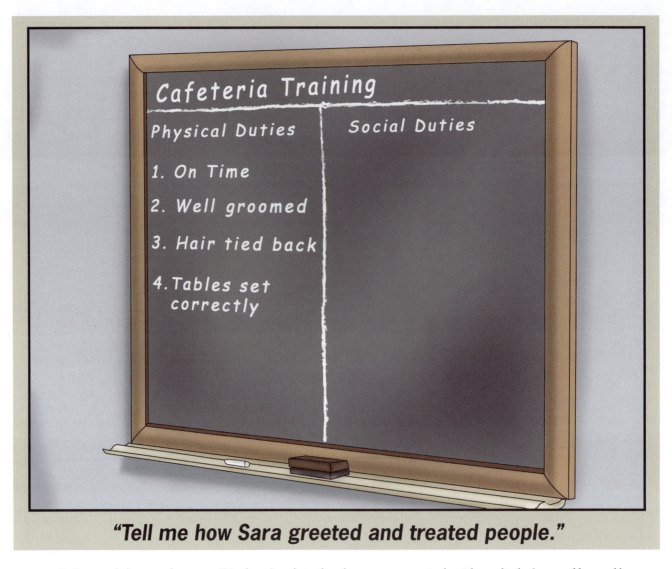

"Tell me how Sara greeted and treated people."

Maria blurted out, "I don't think she was social. She didn't really talk to anyone!"

Shana asked Maria, "Think hard, was Sara rude? Did she ignore people? Did she have a bad attitude?"

"Well, no. She was at her workstation and she looked nice. I liked her uniform. She was neat and clean. That's social responsibility, isn't it?" Maria replied.

Shana nodded in agreement as she said, "Absolutely, Maria. You are correct. Sara was well groomed and dressed appropriately. But you really didn't answer my question yet. Can you tell me how she greeted and treated the people? Think back to when people first sat at one of her tables."

Page 80 | Chapter 13

"Now I've got it."

Maria's face lit up. "Now I've got it. She made eye contact with them and smiled. And when they said thank you for pouring the water, she nodded and answered. Mostly she did her job with a lot of smiling and without talking. Was that good?"

Shana smiled as she said, "Maria, social conversation on your break or after work is different than when you are on the job. While you are working, your employer expects you to do the tasks you have been hired to do, not to spend time chatting with people. Cafeteria employees are expected to smile, to make eye contact and to make people feel comfortable."

"I did not see Sara eat. Doesn't she like food?"

"I have an important question, Shana. What about eating? I did not see Sara eat. Doesn't she like food? I thought cafeteria workers could eat what they want and when they want."

Shana answered with a wide grin, "I know you love to eat, Maria. But I hate to tell you that a cafeteria worker's job is serving food to customers, not eating it herself!"

Questions:

Maria and Shana had a conversation about the way Sara proved she was a good cafeteria worker by.

      a. paying attention   b. making eye contact   c. both a and b

People usually demonstrate interest in a conversation by _____ and by _____ .

1. What did Maria and Shana do after the first cafeteria training session?
2. In what way did Maria feel that Sara showed social responsibility?
3. What might happen in the cafeteria if Sara felt it was her social responsibility to have conversations with all the customers?
4. How can social responsibility be different at work than when you are not working?

An Attitude | Page 83

Vocabulary

spiffy - *attractive, smart looking*
Jerome got a spiffy saddlebag for his bike.

saddlebag - *sack that hangs on something*
The new saddlebag was made of leather.

weird - *odd, strange*
Jerome thought it was weird for James to give him such a gift.

confused - *puzzled, uncertain*
Jerome was confused because Shana seemed angry.

novella

14 Jerome And The Surprise Package
Real Friends

Jerome felt angry with James.

Most of the day, Jerome's Big Red stood outside BIG-BUY, ready and waiting. James had continued to 'borrow' Big Red. In fact, since Jerome had gotten the spiffy leather 'saddlebag', James used the bike even more than before. James did not tell Jerome when he was going to use it. He acted as if it wasn't any of Jerome's business. Jerome felt angry with James. He was beginning to think that James was not a good friend.

"James must have put this package here. Was I wrong about him?"

Jerome was showing Shana the new saddlebag when he found the little package at the bottom of the saddlebag. It was wrapped in plain white paper and tied with green cord. It was a small package that looked like a gift. It had not been there in the morning when he took his lunch out of the saddlebag.

"Hey, Shana, look what I found! James must have put it here. I guess I was wrong about James."

Shana looked on without saying a word.

"This is a weird gift. James knows I don't smoke."

"Gee, I wonder what it could be? Maybe James wanted to surprise me with a thank you gift," Jerome said excitedly.

Shana had a strange look on her face and replied, "Well, perhaps so. Why not open it?"

Jerome pulled the green cord off and tore the white paper away from the package. "Shana, it looks like tobacco in a small plastic bag. This is a weird gift. James knows I don't smoke."

Jerome And The Surprise Package | Page 87

"I think we'd better show this to your manager."

Shana's tone of voice told Jerome that she was angry. "Jerome, I think we'd better show this to your manager, Mr. Daniels." As Shana turned to go to Mr. Daniel's office, she said, "You and I will have to talk a little about this package, real friends and people who pretend to be friends. Then I would like you to come with me to get a new lock for your bike."

Jerome felt confused. What made Shana so angry? Was it the gift or was Shana angry with him? Would Mr. Daniels be angry, too? He did want to talk to Shana about his friends at work, especially James. But why, he wondered, did Shana think he should get a new lock today?

Questions:

Jerome found a gift-wrapped package in his saddlebag. His face showed that he felt:

        a. pleased   b. puzzled   c. angry

When unusual or unexpected things happen to us, we often feel _____ .

1. How did Jerome feel about James always using his bike?
2. What did James find in the saddlebag?
3. What might have happened if Shana had not been with Jerome when he found the surprise package?
4. What do you think was in the package? Do you think it was meant as a gift for Jerome?

Jerome And The Surprise Package

Vocabulary

disease - *illness*
A TV show linked disease to not washing hands after using the bathroom.

decision - *choice*
Maria's decision to wash up brought her to the treasure.

crumpled - *wrinkled*
Someone did not throw the dirty and crumpled towels into the trash.

delicate - *fragile, easily broken*
Maria found a delicate golden bracelet.

treasure - *something of great value or worth*
Maria explained about finding the golden treasure in the bathroom.

novella
15 The Golden Treasure
Respecting The Property Of Others

Maria washed her hands whenever she went into the ladies' room.

Last night, Maria had seen a TV show linking disease to not washing hands after using the bathroom. Right then, she made up her mind to carefully soap and rinse her hands whenever she went to the ladies' room. In fact, it was this decision that brought her to the treasure.

She threw the towels into the basket.

When Maria entered the ladies' room, she noticed a pile of dirty and crumpled paper towels on the counter that someone had not bothered to put into the trash. They made the bathroom look dirty. It annoyed Maria that someone would leave a mess for the next person. She picked up the towels and threw them into the basket. As she tossed them, she heard something fall and hit the floor with a tinkle. Looking down to see what it was, she spotted a shiny object.

"I have always wanted a nice gold bracelet."

Maria bent and picked it up. It was a delicate and lovely gold bracelet. "Oh boy, today's my lucky day," she thought. "I have always wanted a nice gold bracelet. This will go perfectly with my Sunday clothes." Delighted, she put it in her pocket and walked back to her workstation.

All afternoon, as she filed papers, Maria thought about the beautiful gold bracelet in her pocket. She pictured it on her wrist. She pictured people admiring it. She saw herself telling her mom how she had found it.

The Golden Treasure

Maria remembered her mom's voice saying, "IT'S NOT YOURS!"

It was then that she began to feel uncomfortable. Was it her mom's voice she heard telling her that the bracelet belonged to someone else? Was it her mom's voice reminding Maria how she felt when she lost something she loved? Loud and clear, the message kept repeating in her mind, "IT'S NOT YOURS!"

Maria made up her mind. She went to her work coach, Shana, and said, "Can I talk with you about something important?" Shana smiled and asked Maria what the problem was. Maria explained about finding the golden treasure in the bathroom. She admitted that she wanted to keep it but that a little voice kept telling her that it was not hers. She asked Shana, "What shall I do?"

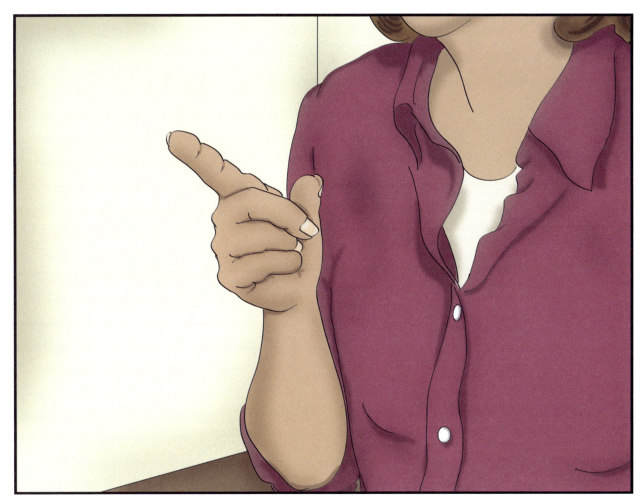

Questions:

Maria pictured her mom pointing a finger as she said, "IT'S NOT YOURS!" The pointing finger showed that mom felt the message was:

        a. important   b. boring   c. silly

We often use our hands to help tell a story. A pointing finger helps us to show that what is being said is _____ .

1. What was the golden treasure that Maria found?
2. How did she find it?
3. How did her mother's voice change Maria's actions?
4. Why was it important that Maria did not keep the golden treasure?

The Golden Treasure | Page 95

Vocabulary

mute - *without sound*
Jerome's cell had spent each day mute, clipped to his belt where he placed it each morning.

displeasure - *anger, disapproval*
The customers groaned their displeasure at Jerome's failure to do his job.

misplaced - *something not where it should be*
Jerome's behavior showed that he had misplaced his loyalty to his job and the customers.

focus - *attention, concentrated effort*
Jerome's focus was on the phone call and not his job.

discourteous - *rude, not polite.*
Jerome plunked the groceries into the cart in a discourteous manner.

novella

16 Misplaced Focus
Cell Phone Etiquette

"Oh, boy! I have a call!"

Jerome was packing a large bag of groceries when he heard the tune of his cell. "Oh, boy! I have a call," Jerome announced as he plunked the groceries into the cart in a discourteous manner. Since James had been fired, Jerome's cell had been silent. It had spent each day mute, clipped to his belt where he placed it each morning.

Misplaced Focus | Page 97

People did not seem happy about his behavior.

Now Jerome unclipped his cell from his belt. He was obviously pleased. Uncertain how loud he needed to talk, his "Hello" carried across the check out lanes.

If Jerome had been watching or listening, he would have noticed that the people waiting in the checkout line did not seem happy about his behavior. Ellie, the cashier, was shocked at Jerome's behavior. She looked at him and shook her head.

Page 98 | Chapter 16

"Come on, Jerome. I'm in a rush."

"Hi, Jerome. This is Alan. Remember me? We were in Shana's training class together." Jerome heard Alan's voice clearly on his cell. So did everyone on the checkout line.

The elderly lady expecting her groceries to be bagged said in an irritated voice, "Come on, Jerome. I'm in a rush." The customers behind her groaned their displeasure as well.

Jerome, however, heard none of that. He was focused on his first real cell phone call. To top that off, it was from his friend Alan. "Gosh, Alan, I'm so glad to hear from you. How did you get my number?"

Jerome chatted as if he had all the time in the world.

Misplaced Focus | Page 99

Groceries were backing up on the counter.

Meantime, Ellie kept right on ringing up prices of the grocery items on the belt. Groceries were backing up on the counter and piling up at Jerome's bagging station. Ellie had an annoyed look on her face. The customers voiced their annoyance at Jerome's behavior to Ellie and to each other.

As if planned, two of the customers called out, "Alan, Jerome is at work. Call him back later." And with that, Ellie turned around to Jerome and firmly stated, "This is not appropriate, Jerome. Call Alan back when you are not working."

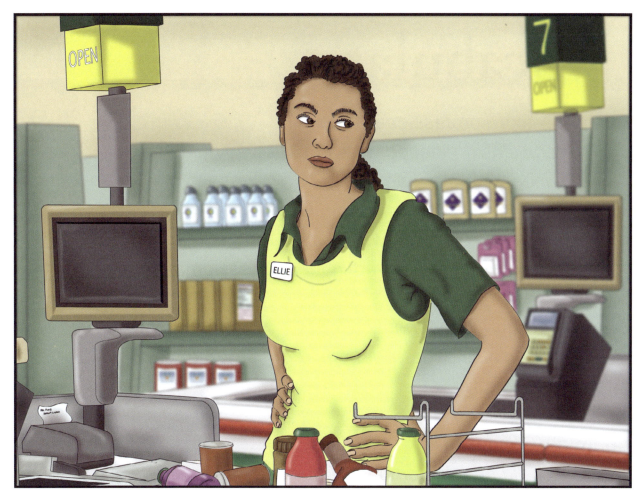

Questions:

Ellie's body language sent a message to Jerome. Her hands on her hips, her frown and her raised eyebrows showed that she was:

        a. annoyed   b. excited   c. surprised

If someone says or does something inappropriate, our body language may show that we are _____.

1. What happened to interrupt Jerome as he was packing groceries?
2. Why were Ellie and the customers annoyed with Jerome?
3. What might have happened if Ellie had not said, "This is not appropriate, Jerome. Call back when you are not working?"
4. How had Jerome's behavior changed the way customers were being treated?

Vocabulary

business-like - *professional, efficient*
Shana's next meeting with Jerome was held in a business-like manner.

expression - *look that shows feeling*
Shana's concern showed in the expression on her face.

questioningly - *wonderingly*
"Mr. Daniels needs your help, too?" Jerome responded questioningly.

complain - *find fault*
"Why did people complain?" Jerome asked almost in tears.

fired - *to have employment ended*
Sometimes customer complaints can cause an employee to be fired.

emergency - *crisis*
Cell phones can be helpful in cases of emergency or for social calls at appropriate times.

novella 17 The Good and the Bad
Appropriate Cell Phone Use

"Yesterday I got a phone call from Mr. Daniels."

Shana's next meeting with Jerome was held in a business-like manner. Her concern showed in the expression on her face. "Jerome, yesterday I got a phone call from Mr. Daniels. He seemed upset and asked if I could help him out."

"Mr. Daniels needs your help too? I thought I was the only one at BIG-BUY that you helped." Jerome responded questioningly.

The Good and the Bad | Page 103

Mr. Daniels got several complaints about your work yesterday.

"Usually, that is the case but this time Mr. Daniels needs help concerning you. He said that he had gotten several complaints about your work yesterday. He told me that when customers complain to the manager about an employee, the manager must try to eliminate the cause of the complaints. Sometimes that means firing an employee."

"Now I remember. I got a call from Alan."

"Oh, no! I'm going to be fired? I thought I was a good worker. I report on time. I try to do my best. Why did people complain?" Jerome asked almost in tears.

"Think back to yesterday while you were bagging groceries on Ellie's line. Do you remember anything unusual that happened?" Shana asked encouragingly.

For a moment Jerome was puzzled; then it dawned on him. "Yesterday I got a cell call from Alan. Could that be the problem?"

"Indeed, Jerome. Cell phones can be helpful in cases of emergency or for social calls at appropriate times."

"Jerome, what do you think you should say to Mr. Daniels?"

Shana continued, "Social conversations should take place in free time, not when they interfere with work and not when they might bother other people. What do you think you should do about Mr. Daniels? How will you prevent another cell phone problem from developing?"

Thinking over what Shana had said, Jerome asked, "Shana, can cell phones be both good and bad? Will you help me figure out when and where I can use my new cell phone so I don't get in more trouble?"

Questions:

Jerome's body language and facial expression showed that he was:

        a. upset   b. happy   c. proud

If employees make a mistake at work and they have to talk to their boss, their body language and facial expressions may show they are _____.

    1. Who called Shana asking for help?

    2. What did Jerome do that caused Mr. Daniels to be upset?

    3. What might have happened if Shana did not talk to Jerome about using his cell phone at work?

    4. How can using a cell phone at work cause a problem for employees and customers?

The Good and the Bad | Page 107

Vocabulary

crisis - *disaster*
Maria had a lunchtime crisis when she avoided completing her job responsibilities.

critical - *serious, significant*
Shana needed to talk to Maria about a critical job she was supposed to finish.

responsible - *dependable, accountable*
Being a responsible employee sometimes means putting what you want to do after what your employer needs you to do.

starved - *very hungry*
Maria was absolutely starved.

crimson - *deep red color*
Her face turned crimson.

novella

18 Lunchtime Crisis
Avoiding Job Responsibilities

"**Please be certain to get all those papers filed before lunch.**"

Maria's job coach, Shana, called to her, "Maria, you are doing an especially important job today. Many people are depending on you. Please be certain to get all those papers filed before lunch. In fact, why don't you take a late lunch so you can get this work finished?"

Lunchtime Crisis | Page 109

"Those papers can wait," Maria thought. "I want to eat."

Maria looked at her watch. It was 11:40. Then she looked at the large stack of forms left for filing. "Oh, no. I did not take my break today. I am absolutely starved. 12:00 is my lunchtime and I need my lunch."

Maria continued to work. She managed to get several more papers filed. Again she looked at her watch. It was a few minutes before noon, her lunchtime. There was still a small stack of papers left to do.

"Those papers can wait," Maria thought. "I want to eat."

She put her favorites on her tray and paid the cashier.

Maria slipped very quietly by Shana's office on her way to her locker. She got her wallet and made a quick stop to wash up at the ladies' room. Then she headed down to the cafeteria.

"Boy, it's crowded today," she thought. "Good thing I have friends to sit with." Maria got at the end of the lunch line and looked at the several food offerings. She put her favorites on her tray and paid the cashier. Taking her tray, she headed to a table where her friends were seated and sat down to enjoy her lunch.

Lunchtime Crisis | Page 111

"Maria, I need to talk to you…"

Maria was two bites into her sandwich when Shana came into the cafeteria. She headed toward Maria and stopped by her side. "Maria, I need to talk to you about a critical job you were supposed to finish."

Maria's stomach dropped like a rock. Her appetite left her. Her face turned crimson. She recalled yesterday's work lesson on completing assigned jobs. She remembered Shana saying, "Being a responsible employee sometimes means putting what you want to do after what your employer needs you to do."

Questions:

Maria's face turned crimson when Shana came to the cafeteria to talk to her about not completing the critical job. Maria felt:

        a. excited   b. pleased   c. embarrassed

When an employer talks to us about a job we failed to do or about inappropriate behavior, our faces may turn red showing that we feel _____.

1. What did Shana ask Maria to do before she went to lunch?
2. What did Maria decide to do at lunchtime?
3. How can failing to do a critical job affect coworkers?
4. Why is it important to complete assigned jobs to the best of your ability?

Lunchtime Crisis | Page 113

Vocabulary

evaluating - *figure out the value or worth of something*
Employers try to help employees improve job performance by evaluating their work habits.

mumbled - *talking in an unclear way, hard to understand*
Maria mumbled, "Did I make a poor choice today?"

conflicting - *disagreeing, difference of opinion*
It is sometimes difficult to decide how best to handle conflicting needs.

adviser - *someone who gives advice or assistance*
An adviser or trusted friend can help when you are unsure of what to do.

depending - *counting on someone or something*
Your coworkers are depending upon you to complete your job.

improve - *to make better*
Good workers are always looking for ways to improve.

relieved - *calmed, feel better*
After the conversation with Shana, Maria had a relieved look on her face.

novella

19 Room for Improvement
Evaluating Work Habits

"Did I make a poor choice today?"

Maria was seated in Shana's office. She felt confused and uncertain as she thought back on her morning. Shana, her job coach, seemed disappointed in her.

Shana came in and eased her wheelchair under her desk opposite Maria. With a serious look on her face, she asked, "What happened this morning, Maria? Let's talk."

Maria mumbled, "Did I make poor choices today? But what should I have done?"

Room for Improvement | Page 115

"Perhaps you did not understand how to handle the conflicting needs."

"Two excellent questions, Maria. Perhaps you did not understand how to handle the conflicting needs, yours for lunch and mine for the completion of your assigned job. That is not unusual. Many times employees find that they are unsure what to do. The good news is that you admitted you were confused and now want to find out what you could have done differently."

Maria sat quietly. She seemed to be thinking about what she had done and about what Shana said.

"I am upset that I did not please you."

Maria barely looked up when she murmured, "I am upset that I did not please you. I want to be a responsible worker. I want to be someone that you can count on."

"That's exactly what I want for you, Maria," Shana responded. "Often workers who are unsure of how best to do something turn to a trusted friend or adviser for help. You can turn to me, your job coach, with your questions. Together, we should be able to find answers."

Room for Improvement | Page 117

Shana handed Maria a tissue.

Shana continued, "This morning you went to lunch without completing an important task that I had told you was critical. It would have been better for both of us if you had come to me and asked for help. What you do or don't do on the job affects other people and their work. You are part of a work team."

Maria felt rotten. She took the tissue Shana offered to wipe the tears streaming down her face.

Speaking kindly, Shana said, "Do not be too upset, Maria. It is wise to learn from mistakes. At some time, we all make them. Good workers are always looking for ways to improve!"

"Thank you, Shana. I'll try to do better," Maria said with a relieved look on her face.

Questions:

Shana explained that Maria's decision not to complete the critical job affected other people. Maria's face and her slumped body position showed that she felt:

      a. bored   b. annoyed   c. upset

Disappointing other people by failing to follow through on a responsibility usually makes us feel _____ .

1. What two needs caused a problem for Maria?
2. Who might employees turn to for help solving work problems?
3. If Maria had asked Shana for help, what might she have done differently?
4. How can being part of a work team affect how a job is done?

Room for Improvement | Page 119

Vocabulary

workstation - *special place of work*
   Maria's workstation faced the doorway opposite the window.

tumbled - *fell or dropped*
   The files tumbled to the floor.

grumbled - *complained*
   "Cleaning this up and getting things back in order will take forever," Maria grumbled.

responded - *answered*
   "I would really appreciate your help," Maria responded.

relieved - *calmed, feel better*
   Maria was relieved that Bianca came to help her.

novella

20 Help! Papers Everywhere
Accepting Help

"What is that?"

Maria's workstation faced the doorway directly opposite the window. Usually she kept an eye on what was happening in the hall and enjoyed a breeze while filing papers and folders. She made every effort not to talk while she worked even though she wanted to chat with coworkers.

"What was that?" The sound of a loud crash from outside the window startled Maria.

The files tumbled, spilling papers out onto the floor.

Maria turned quickly to look out the window to see what had happened. As she did, her sleeve caught on the stack of files. The files tumbled, spilling papers out onto the floor all around her.

"Oh, no. I don't believe it!" groaned Maria in a voice loud enough to catch the attention of her friend, Bianca, working nearby. Spotting Maria's problem, Bianca rushed over.

"Oh, Bianca. Look at this awful mess. Cleaning this up and getting things back in order will take forever," Maria grumbled.

"Today has not been my best day at work."

"Why don't you let me help you?" Bianca offered.

"Gosh, I certainly would appreciate your help. Could you pick up the papers and files? Then I can sort the papers and put them back in their files," Maria responded with a relieved smile on her face.

"Today has not been my best day at work. That noise startled me so much. I seem to have made a bit of a mess of everything," Maria groaned.

"That's what friends do, help each other."

"Thank you for coming right over to offer to help. Thank you for helping me get this mess cleaned up. It would have taken me a long time without you," Maria admitted.

"That's okay, Maria. I was glad to help you. After all, we do work together. That's what friends do, help each other," Bianca remarked.

The friends worked together. Before too long, the papers and files were sorted and back on Maria's workstation.

Questions:

Maria heard a loud crash from outside the window. Her face showed that she was:

      a. excited   b. startled   c. annoyed

When an unexpected event occurs, our faces and body language may show we are: _____ .

1. How did the location of Maria's workstation cause a problem?
2. In what way did Bianca assist Maria with her problem?
3. What could have resulted if Maria did not accept Bianca's offer to help?
4. How did Maria show her appreciation to Bianca for helping her?

Help! Papers Everywhere | Page 125

Vocabulary

window shopping - *looking at things but not buying*
    Sometimes Maria and her mother went window shopping at the State Street Mall.

independence - *able to care for one's self*
    Maria had a great feeling of independence from traveling on her own to and from work.

confidently - *certain or sure way of behaving*
    Maria marched into work confidently.

anxiety - *uneasiness, concern*
    "What am I supposed to do and where am I supposed to do it?" Maria asked with some anxiety in her voice.

novella

21 Unexpected Changes
Requesting Information

Sometimes Maria and Bianca listened to their CDs.

Weekends always seemed to speed by. Yes, there were so many choices to make about how to spend their 'free' time on the weekends.

Sometimes Maria and Bianca listened to favorite CDs. Other times, Maria and her mom went window shopping at the State Street Mall.

Unexpected Changes | Page 127

Maria traveled on her own.

Nonetheless, Maria noticed that by Sunday evening she was getting anxious to return to another week at work. There was a great feeling of independence that came with traveling to and from work on her own.

Once at work, Maria liked the security of the routines that filled her workday. She liked having her own workspace, her own job responsibilities and being trusted to follow through on her work. Most of all, she loved the feeling of being part of the work team and making new friends.

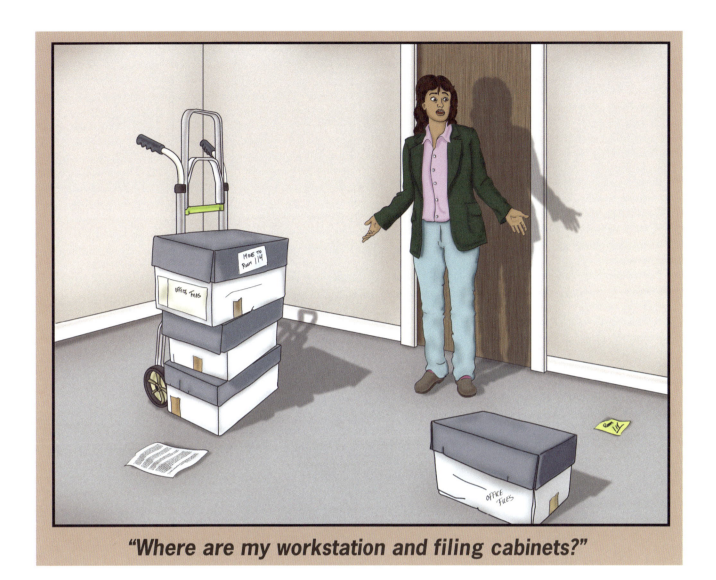

"Where are my workstation and filing cabinets?"

Maria was excited and pleased to start a brand new work week. She breezed through her sign-in routines and walked purposefully to deposit her backpack in her locker. Then, she headed to her work area.

"Oh, no. What happened here? Now what?" Maria blurted in an upset manner. "Where are my workstation and my file cabinets? I had better find out what is going on. Who shall I ask?" she wondered on the verge of tears.

Unexpected Changes | Page 129

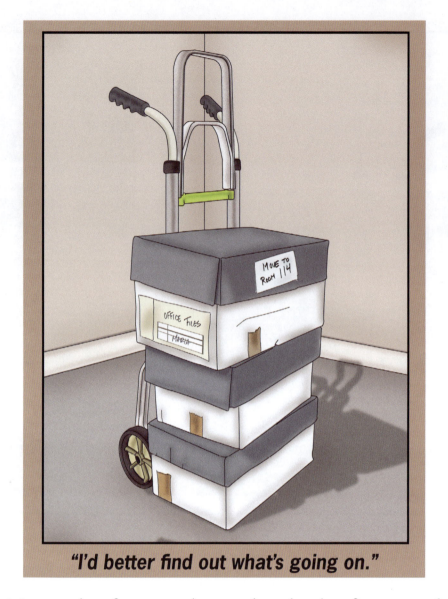
"I'd better find out what's going on."

It took Maria only a few seconds to realize that her feet seemed to know the answer. They were taking her to Shana, her job coach. Fortunately, Shana was in her office and not busy.

"Hi, Shana. I am so upset. Did I do something wrong? Have I been fired?" Maria questioned with panic in her voice.

"Fired? Maria, why would you think such a thing?" Shana asked.

"Please, Shana, could you come with me? I'll show you. I hope you can figure out what's going on because I can't. If I'm not fired, can you tell me what happened? What am I supposed to do and where am I supposed to do it?" Maria asked with some anxiety in her voice.

Questions:

Maria found that her workstation and filing cabinets were missing. Her wide-open eyes, mouth, arms and hands showed her great:

      a. pleasure   b. shyness   c. shock

Our faces and bodies often tell a story before we speak. When the unexpected occurs, our faces and body language may show _____ .

1. Describe how Maria felt on Sunday evening.
2. What were two things that Maria liked about going to work?
3. What upsetting thing did Maria find when she went to her work area?
4. Why was it a wise decision for Maria to see Shana about her concerns?

Unexpected Changes | Page 131

Vocabulary

responded - *answered*
Maria responded in a soft but clear voice.

conference - *meeting or discussion*
The conference for Shana will be tomorrow.

purpose - *the reason*
"Call Ms. Walden to discuss the purpose of the meeting."

commented - *mentioned, remarked*
"Please give Shana the message as soon as she returns," Ms. Walden commented.

difficulty - *situation that causes a problem*
Shana and Maria were talking about yesterday's difficulty.

novella

22 Did I Get That Right?
Taking A Message

Maria and Shana were talking when the phone rang.

Maria and Shana were sitting in Shana's office chatting about yesterday's difficulty when the phone rang. After a brief conversation, Shana got up and walked to the door.

"Maria, why don't you stay here and go over the charts we made on cafeteria work? I have been called out to solve a small problem. I should not be long."

Did I Get That Right? | Page 133

"Hello, Ms. Walden."

It seemed only a minute later that the 'Big Boss' stopped by. Tall and ever so attractive in her neat blue suit, Ms. Walden walked right into Shana's office. "Hi, Maria. I'm looking for Shana," she said.

A little nervous at answering the 'Big Boss', Maria softly but clearly responded, "Hello, Ms. Walden. Shana was just called out. She should be back soon. Can I give her a message?"

"Why, yes, that would be nice," Ms. Walden agreed.

"Please let me find a pen and pad so I can write it down. I want to get your message right," Maria said grabbing a pen and pad from the corner of the desk. "Now I am ready."

Page 134 | Chapter 22

Maria repeated the message aloud as she wrote it.

Ms. Walden began slowly, "Please tell Shana that our conference will be held tomorrow, Tuesday, at 5:30 p.m. in my office."

Maria wrote as quickly as she could, repeating the message aloud while she wrote it. When she had finished, she looked up and asked, "Ms. Walden, please may I read it back to you just to make certain that I have it right? I don't want to make a mistake."

Did I Get That Right? | Page 135

"Ms. Walden, may I read it back to you?"

Ms. Walden continued, "Please do, Maria. Would you also ask her to give me a call? We need to discuss the purpose of the meeting."

As Ms. Walden turned to leave, Maria wrote the last part of the message.

"Good-bye, Maria, and thank you. I would appreciate it if you would give her the message as soon as she returns," Ms. Walden commented while walking out of the room.

Questions:

Maria's big boss, Ms. Walden, arrived when Shana was not there. Maria's face showed that she felt:

      a. delighted   b. confident   c. nervous

Meeting with employers or people in positions of authority can make us feel unsure and _____ .

1. Who was Maria's 'Big Boss'?
2. How did Maria feel about talking to her 'Big Boss'?
3. What might have happened if Maria had not written the message down?
4. How did Maria make certain that the message she planned to give Shana was correct?

Did I Get That Right? | Page 137

Vocabulary

distracted - *not focused*
Alan smiled but looked a bit distracted.

relief - *a break, a feeling of release from stress*
Relief and pleasure showed on Alan's face when Maria offered to show him how to ride the bus.

fare - *amount of money charged for a journey*
The bus fare is one dollar if you have a reduced fare pass.

reduced - *became smaller in size or made simpler*
The reduced fare pass saves you money each time you take the bus.

novella
23 Sharing An Adventure
Giving Help And Sharing Information

"I ride the public bus to and from work."

Alan saw Maria again at their afternoon break. Alan smiled but looked a bit distracted. "Maria, does your mom pick you up every day after work?" Alan asked.

"Oh, no. I ride the public bus to and from work. I want to be independent," Maria replied.

"You know how to do everything."

"I would really like to do that, too," Alan responded. He took a deep breath and said, "But I don't think I can. I live way out on Pine Street. Where do you live?"

"For Heaven's sake, I live around the corner! I live on Oak Street. Maybe we can ride the bus together," Maria answered excitedly.

Relief and pleasure showed on Alan's face as he continued, "I knew it. I just knew you were brave. You seem to know how to do everything that I still have to learn."

Maria's smile showed that she felt pleased with Alan's comments.

"Wait, I have an idea."

"It is so much fun to ride the bus, Alan. You're going to love it. Oh, do you have a reduced fare bus pass?" Maria asked, forgetting her shyness altogether.

Alan grinned, "Yep, that's one thing I did right. Mom took me to get one last week."

Maria went on, "You will need your pass and one dollar because we are outside the city limits. Wait, I have an idea." Maria dashed to her workstation and grabbed a pen and a pad of paper; then hurried back to join Alan.

Sharing An Adventure | Page 141

"Let's make a prompt card for you."

"Let's make a prompt card for you for tomorrow," Maria said cheerfully. She then wrote the following instructions:

1. Meet Maria at 7:30 a.m. at the corner of Pine Street and Oak Street.
2. Bring reduced fare pass and a dollar for each way on the bus.
3. Walk to bus stop.
4. Take the N19 bus to Center Street.
5. Check for your belongings and get off the bus.

After finishing the card, Maria turned to Alan and exclaimed, "If you have any questions tomorrow, I'll answer them while we are on our bus adventure!"

Alan grinned. Relief and pleasure showed on his face.

Questions:

Maria offered to make Alan a prompt card and to ride the public bus with him to work. Alan's face and hands showed that he felt:

      a. angry   b. relieved   c. sad

An offer of help to do something that is new or uncomfortable for us makes us feel _____ .

1. How did Maria get to work each day?
2. Why did Alan call Maria brave?
3. How did Maria help Alan become more independent?
4. How is a prompt card helpful in new situations?

Sharing An Adventure | Page 143

Vocabulary

compliment - *to praise, to say a kind thing*
Shana gave Maria a compliment about the recent things she had done to help Alan.

drifting - *wandering*
Maria's mind began drifting off as she pictured herself working in the cafeteria wearing a cute uniform.

nervousness - *jumpiness, stress*
A feeling of nervousness began to replace Maria's feeling of excitement.

observing - *watching, viewing*
Shana had been observing some things Maria had done.

journey - *a trip*
Maria said that now she had Alan to share her bus journey to work.

novella

24 Good Stuff

Receiving a Compliment

Maria pictured herself working in a cute uniform.

Maria filed the papers as quickly as possible. Yesterday Shana had promised her another training lesson for cafeteria work if she was able to complete this job before class time. It looked like she would be finished in time. Maria found her mind drifting off. She pictured herself working in the cafeteria wearing a cute uniform.

Good Stuff | Page 145

A feeling of nervousness began to replace a feeling of excitement.

"Good morning, Maria," Shana said as she stopped by Maria's workstation. Please come to my office as soon as you finish. I have something important that I need to share with you."

"Sure, Shana," Maria replied. Her high hopes dropped. Had she messed up again? Would Shana cancel the cafeteria training? A feeling of nervousness began to replace her feeling of excitement. Maria worried all the way to Shana's office.

Maria noticed that the door to Shana's office was open. She waited outside for a moment trying to get up enough courage to go in.

"Maybe I'm not in trouble."

Shana was seated at her desk. She looked at Maria and smiled, "Come in. Sit down."

Maria was puzzled. Shana had a big smile and her voice sounded friendly. "Maybe I'm not in trouble," Maria thought.

"Maria, I want you to know that I have been observing some things that you have done recently. You have gone out of your way to help Alan. You have helped him learn work routines. Also, he told me that you are teaching him to travel to and from work on the public bus. He seems to think you know everything there is to know! I'm proud of you. You are acting like Alan's job coach!"

"I am proud of you, Maria."

Maria's face broke out into a big grin, "Oh, thank you, Shana. Guess what? I like helping people. Alan is funny and nice. And now I have someone to share my bus journey to work. Maybe one day I'll be a job coach, just like you."

Shana continued, "I am proud of you, Maria. You have become a good employee."

Maria could have floated out of Shana's office. "Wait 'til I tell Mom this good stuff," she thought.

Questions:

Maria heard Shana's compliment. Shana's smile and thumbs up sign meant:

         a. trouble   b. good work   c. bad news

When we are pleased with someone, we may smile and give a thumb's up sign to show _____ .

1. What did Shana say when she stopped by Maria's workstation?
2. How did Maria feel about Shana's request?
3. What compliment did Shana give Maria?
4. How did Maria respond to the good news?

Good Stuff | Page 149

Vocabulary

complained - *grumbled, criticized*
People complained to my boss about me.

holidays - *special days*
My family has parties on birthdays and other holidays.

supposed to - *to be expected to do something*
I'm not supposed to talk on my cell phone during work.

novella
25 The Invitation
Social Behavior

"Hello, this is Jerome. May I speak to Alan, please?"

"Hello, this is Jerome. May I speak with Alan, please?" Jerome spoke clearly into the phone. He listened as a woman, maybe Alan's mother, called Alan and asked him to answer the phone. He heard Alan pick up.

"Hello, Jerome. You decided to call me this time!" Alan responded.

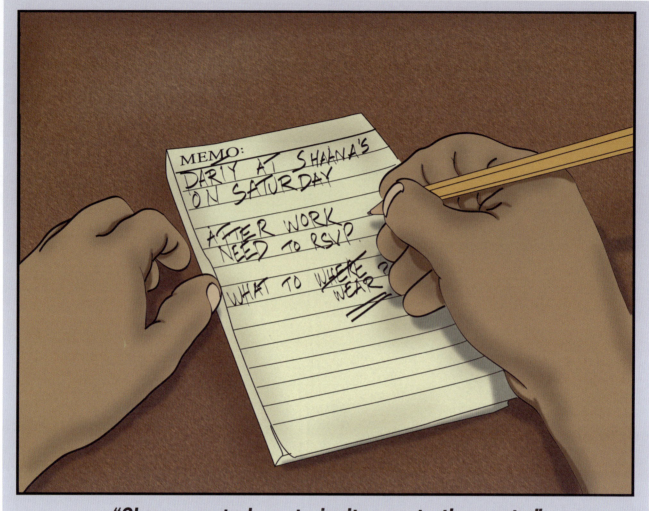

"Shana wanted me to invite you to the party."

"Hi, Alan. Yes, I am calling from my home phone. You know what? I got in a lot of trouble the other day when you called. I'm not supposed to talk on my cell phone during work. I didn't know that. People complained to my boss about me. No more cell phone calls for me at work. I don't want to get fired."

"Sorry about that, Jerome. I wasn't thinking about your job. I was excited about talking to you. That's all I had on my mind. Shana wanted me to invite you to the party. I never did get to ask you before that lady told you to hang up."

"When is the party? Will there be girls?"

"Party? I love parties, especially if there is lots of food. My family has parties for everyone's birthday and on holidays. Are you having a party?" Jerome asked excitedly.

"No, Jerome, I'm not having a party," Alan explained. "Shana is having a get-together for all of her job trainees and she wanted me to invite you to come."

"Gosh, that sounds great," Jerome responded. "But when is it? Will there be girls? What will I wear? What will I say? How will I get there?"

"Can I go with you? I don't know how to talk to girls."

"Take it slow, Jerome. I can't focus on all of those questions at once. You had better ask them one at a time. I think you have too many questions for me to answer."

Jerome continued as if he had not heard Alan. "You know what, Alan? I'm already getting nervous. I've never been to a 'friends' party. What if I don't know what to do or say? Can I go with you? I don't know how to talk to girls. Do you have a girl friend?" Jerome asked.

Questions:

The expression on Jerome's face, as he looked into the mirror to fix his hair, showed that he felt:

        a. tired   b. trapped   c. pleased

Receiving an invitation makes us feel _____ because it shows that someone likes our company.

1. Whom did Jerome phone?
2. Why did Jerome tell Alan that he could not use his cell phone for calls at work?
3. What did Alan ask Jerome?
4. What did Jerome say that told you how he felt about the invitation?

The Invitation | Page 155

Vocabulary

casual - *relaxed, informal*
Some of the outfits were too casual for work.

bored - *uninterested*
Bianca had tried on so many outfits that she was getting tired and Maria was getting bored.

exchange - *to swap, change places*
The department store had a good exchange policy if clothing needed to be returned.

refund - *money back*
The department store would give a refund if something did not fit or was not what the customer wanted.

immediately - *right away, now*
Maria had to leave immediately in order to get home by 5 p.m.

twirled - *whirled, spun*
Bianca twirled around to show off her new, green outfit.

novella 26 Looking Good

Giving a Compliment

Bianca tried on what seemed like millions of outfits.

Bianca and Maria spent most of Saturday at the mall trying to find a new work outfit for Bianca. They went into store after store. Bianca tried on what seemed like a million outfits. Some were too tight, some too dressy, some too casual and some just looked terrible. Bianca was getting tired of taking off her clothes and trying on possible new stuff. Maria was getting bored.

Looking Good | Page 157

Bianca found and bought a green, two-piece outfit.

Bianca made up her mind to buy the next outfit she really liked and to take it home to try it. She knew that the department store had a good return policy for exchange or a refund. Almost as soon as she had decided not to try any more on at the store, Bianca found and bought a green, two-piece outfit. Maria barely had time to see it before the clerk put it in the bag and handed it to Bianca.

Of course, Maria was dying to see the outfit on Bianca. They hurried back to Bianca's house for a mini fashion show. Unfortunately, when Maria checked the time, she realized that she had to leave Bianca's immediately in order to be home by five. She was greatly disappointed.

The green outfit was draped on the hanger.

Maria hated to miss out on the showing but her mom was strict. Five o'clock meant just that, five o'clock. Maria took one last look before rushing out. She admired the green outfit draped on the hanger. In her mind, she pictured Bianca modeling it.

The next day, Maria spotted Bianca at the sign-in counter wearing the new green outfit. Maria rushed up to her and said excitedly, "Oh, Bianca, what a great choice you made. I'm glad you waited to get this outfit. How do you like it?"

"TA DUM! I love it."

Bianca checked that no one was around except Maria, then announced, "TA DUM!" and twirled once in front of the punch-in area. "I love it."

"That outfit is perfect for work. It looks to me that you picked out a winner, Bianca. That green color is perfect! I really think you look great in it," Maria added.

"Thanks. I'm so glad you think so. I'll let you know later if it's comfortable for working," Bianca responded, looking mighty pleased.

With that, the two friends walked away from the sign-in counter and over to the time clock to punch-in.

Page 160 | Chapter 26

Questions:

Bianca showed off her new outfit to Maria. What did her face and body language tell about how she felt about her new clothes?

      a. delighted   b. discouraged   c. annoyed

Being well groomed and wearing appropriate clothes feels good. If someone compliments us we feel _____ .

1. For what reason were Bianca and Maria at the mall?
2. Why didn't Maria stay for the mini fashion show?
3. What was Maria's compliment to Bianca?
4. How might giving compliments improve the work environment?

Looking Good | Page 161

Vocabulary

worth - *has value*
Maria felt that her dream was worth sharing.

convincing - *believable*
What reason could Maria give that would be convincing?

opinion - *personal view*
Maria felt Shana would be honest with her opinion.

suggestion - *idea, plan*
Maria had an important suggestion to share.

medical - *having to do with medicine or health*
The TV medical program talked about the importance of hand washing.

campaign - *a plan of action*
Maria said, "I think we should start a hand washing campaign."

novella 27 The Dream

Making a Suggestion

The dream had seemed so real.

Usually Maria slept soundly and resisted getting up. Not today. Today she had awakened well before the alarm clock. She knew why. It was because of the dream. She lay in bed thinking it over. It had seemed so real. She felt certain that it was worth sharing. But to whom would she share it? What reasons could she give that would be convincing?

She didn't want to forget anything.

Maria thought about it as she ate breakfast. She picked up a pencil and began to write her ideas down on a slip of paper. She didn't want to forget anything. She thought all the way to the bus stop. She was so busy thinking that she barely talked to Alan on the bus ride to work.

By the time she had signed in and punched her time card, she had made a decision. The first person she would tell would be Shana. She thought, "I know Shana better than any of the other bosses. It will be good to practice getting my ideas in order. Also, I can count on Shana to be honest with her opinion."

"Shana, I have an important suggestion to share."

Promptly, Maria headed over to Shana's office. She was earlier than usual. Shana, clearly surprised to see Maria, invited her in.

"Shana, I have an important suggestion to share. Do you have a few moments?"

"Absolutely," Shana replied. "I always try to have time for you."

"I have an idea that I think could be helpful. In fact, I think my idea could cut down on sick leave days. I think it could help keep people healthy."

The Dream | Page 165

"I thought about the TV program I saw on hand washing."

Maria looked straight at Shana and continued speaking in a clear voice. "Remember, Shana, how you said that flu season has started? Well, I thought about that and about the TV medical program I saw last week on hand washing. The doctors said that one of the best ways to keep from spreading sickness is to wash our hands."

Taking a breath, Maria went on, "I think we should start a hand washing campaign. We should remind all employees to wash up well with soap and warm water before leaving the restrooms. We could put funny colorful signs in each of the bathrooms. I can write to the TV station to get posters. We could even put a reminder poster by the time clock. What do you think? Is it a good idea?" Maria asked, as she looked at Shana anxiously.

Questions:

Maria made a suggestion that she thought would cut down on the spread of sickness. As she described her plan, her face showed that she was:

        a. lost   b. tired   c. thoughtful

When we share ideas and suggestions that are important to us, we are _____ about what we say.

1. At what time did Maria wake up?
2. Why did Maria feel that she had awakened early?
3. Why did Maria want to share her idea with Shana?
4. How could Maria's idea make a positive difference at work?

The Dream | Page 167

Vocabulary

admitted - *confessed, owned up*
Maria admitted that Alan was the reason she looked forward to her bus trip to work.

comfortable - *at ease, relaxed*
Maria felt comfortable talking with Alan.

embarrassed - *uncomfortable*
Maria felt nervous and embarrassed talking to most boys.

definitely - *without doubt, with no exceptions*
The shirt is in but the shoes definitely have to go.

novella
28 An Unkind Remark
Social Behavior

Maria was getting more comfortable talking to Alan.

As much as Maria had always enjoyed her bus trip to work, she really looked forward to it now. The reason, Maria admitted, was Alan. She and Alan met at the corner of Pine and Oak Streets each morning to walk to the bus stop. Maria was getting more comfortable talking to Alan. She did not feel nervous and embarrassed with him like she did with most other boys. In fact, she thought that he was becoming a friend instead of just a coworker.

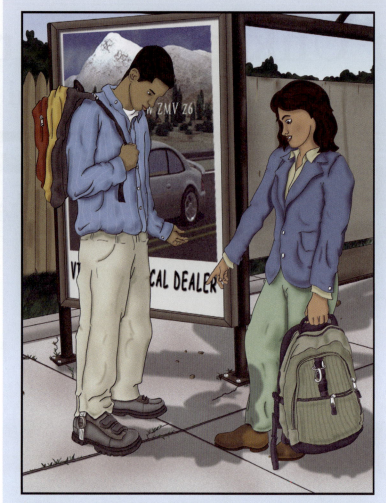

"Those shoes look like 'monster' shoes."

"Hey, Maria, what's happening today?" Alan asked. Alan always smiled. He always had a friendly greeting that made Maria feel special. Also, he seemed to know when to talk and when to listen.

"Hi Alan. Isn't it a great day?" Maria responded. "You know, Alan, you look nice today. I like that blue striped shirt." Then, before really thinking, Maria added, "But those shoes look like 'monster' shoes. You always wear them. How can you wear something so ugly?"

"I heard you, Maria."

Alan's smile disappeared. He said nothing as they continued to walk toward the bus stop.

Maria was uncertain if he had heard her. If he did, why didn't he answer? "Alan, I said the shirt is in, but the shoes definitely have to go."

"I heard you, Maria. Yes, my shoes do look like 'monster' shoes. I hate them. Every morning when I put them on, I wish I had others."

"Couldn't you use your paycheck and save toward some new ones?" Maria asked.

"No, I can't," Alan said in a sad voice. "When I was little I had to have operations on my feet. Doctors say I have to wear these shoes for support. I have no choice."

An Unkind Remark | Page 171

"If I want to walk… I have to wear these shoes."

"Well, those doctors should try wearing those shoes and then maybe they would say something different. Do they think it's funny making you wear those 'monster' shoes? Why don't you tell them you're sick of the costume and it's time for normal shoes?" Maria continued, trying to make certain that Alan got her point.

"Maria, did you hear me?" Alan's voice was very low and sad. "You're lucky. You have a choice. But for me, if I want to walk, which I do, I have to wear these shoes."

Questions:

Maria pointed out that Alan's shoes looked like 'monster' shoes. Alan's face and posture gave Maria a message of:

        a. happiness   b. delight   c. sadness

When people make fun of a disability that we have and cannot change, we often feel and show _____ .

    1. What did Maria particularly like about being with Alan?

    2. What did Maria say that caused Alan's smile to disappear?

    3. Why was it necessary for Alan to wear the 'monster' shoes?

    4. How can unkind remarks affect coworkers and the work environment?

An Unkind Remark | Page 173

Vocabulary

aisle - *a passageway between rows of seats*
Maria looked over at Alan seated across the aisle from her on the bus.

apology - *writing or saying sorry for something said or done*
If Maria wanted to be a real friend, she needed to make an apology to Alan.

blurt - *to speak out without thinking*
Maria asked herself, "Why do I always blurt out something before I think?"

noticed - *observed, saw*
Maria noticed that Alan did not have his usual smile.

silent - *quiet*
Alan was silent during the entire bus ride to work.

deed - *something done on purpose*
Maria realized that she had not been a friend in deed to Alan.

novella
29 The THINK Test
Giving an Apology

"I bet it's what I said about his shoes."

Maria looked over at Alan seated across the aisle from her on the bus. He had decided to sit alone today. Also, she noticed he did not have his usual smile. He was awfully quiet. "Oh, no. What have I done? Has my mouth caused me trouble again? Why do I always blurt out something before I think? I bet it's what I said about his shoes," Maria thought.

The THINK Test | Page 175

He was silent on the bus ride to work.

Alan said nothing to her about operations or 'monster' shoes. In fact, Maria noticed that he was silent the entire bus ride to work. Perhaps he didn't talk because it was hard to talk with their seats separated by the aisle. Or, maybe Alan felt really hurt. Maria was certain that if someone said something unkind to her, she would speak her mind and let them know how she felt.

All day, Maria's mind wandered back to the brief conversation about the 'monster' shoes. She tried to excuse her comments. She thought, "I was trying to be a good friend. I wanted Alan to get some cool shoes that went better with his clothes."

"If it does not pass the THINK test, Maria, don't say it."

But, more and more, her mother's THINK slogan kept popping up. Her mother always told her, "When you're not sure whether to say something, give it the THINK test. Ask yourself if what you have to say is Thoughtful, Honest, Intelligent, Necessary and Kind. If it does not pass the THINK test, Maria, don't say it."

Maria realized that her comments about the 'monster' shoes failed the THINK test. Maybe her failure to think meant that she had failed the friend test. If she wanted to be Alan's friend, she needed to apologize to him. Not one to waste time, Maria decided that now was the time.

"Alan, I want to apologize for what I said."

Maria and Alan shared a common break time and that gave Maria the perfect opportunity. She turned to Alan. In one big burst she said, "Alan, I want to apologize for what I said about the 'monster' shoes. My mouth works faster than my brain. Anyway, look at me. Who am I to tell anyone what to wear? Mom says my choice in colors makes it look like I am colorblind. I am sorry if I made you feel bad."

Alan put down his drink and looked at Maria. A smile broke out on his face. Maria felt relieved and happy to see the usual Alan smile. She grinned widely in return.

Page 178 | Chapter 29

Questions:

Alan's quiet behavior and the serious look on his face showed that he was:

      a. selfish   b. successful   c. hurt

Unkind remarks about the way a person looks or acts cause _____ feelings.

1. What was different about the bus ride that Alan and Maria shared to work?
2. How did Maria try to explain her unkind comments to Alan?
3. How did Maria's words fail the 'THINK' test?
4. What did Maria decide she needed to do to save the friendship?

Vocabulary

RSVP - *answer yes or no to an invitation*
Mom says that polite people RSVP to an invitation.

expert - *a person who knows a lot about something; a specialist*
Alan said that he was not an expert about parties.

host - *a person who invites others to be his guest*
Guests who RSVP help the host know how many people will attend.

etiquette - *rules of polite behavior*
Alan and Jerome wanted to learn about party etiquette.

polite - *showing good manners*
Parties are more fun when guests are polite to each other.

confusion - *misunderstanding facts or a situation*
Jerome's face showed confusion when Alan first mentioned RSVP.

novella
30 Doing the RSVP Thing
Social Etiquette

"Mom says that polite people RSVP."

Alan and Jerome were fishing on their day off. They also were doing a lot of talking. Mostly, they were talking about Shana's party invitation. It was during their conversation that Alan brought up the RSVP.

Alan said, "My mom told me that we need to call Shana and do something she calls RSVP. Mom says that polite people RSVP. I asked mom what RSVP was. She says RSVP is something people do when they are invited to a party or special get-together."

"What will we do to RSVP?"

"What? I don't get it," Jerome's voice and face showed confusion. "What will we do to RSVP and how will we do it?" Jerome asked.

"Mom says that people who RSVP call or write a note telling whether or not they will attend. That way the host will know how many guests to prepare for," Alan continued.

Jerome suggested, "Okay. RSVP doesn't sound too hard. I bet it's so they have enough food. That's important. Let's do this RSVP so Shana won't run out of food at the party."

Page 182 | Chapter 30

"How am I supposed to act?"

Jerome continued, "You know, Alan, I have lots more stuff to learn about parties. I mean, when I go to a 'friend party', how am I supposed to act? You always seem to know what to say. But me, I'm a little afraid that I won't be able to think of anything to say."

Alan responded, "Hey, Jerome. Mom always tells me to keep it simple and smile. She says that a smile can say more than a whole lot of words."

"Yeah, I like people who smile. Shana almost always smiles. I like to smile. But after I smile, what do I do?"

Doing the RSVP Thing | Page 183

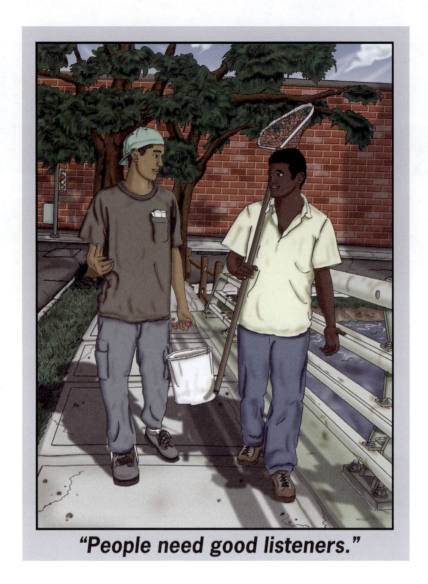

"People need good listeners."

"Have you been to a lot of parties, Alan? You seem to know a lot about what to do," Jerome continued.

"No, Jerome. Believe me, I'm no expert at all. My mom sometimes tells me helpful stuff. She says most people like to talk about themselves, if they have a good listener. She says if I ask a question about what they do, they'll talk. Then I won't have to worry about what to say. I tried it at work and she was right!"

Questions:

Jerome turned to face Alan. The look on Jerome's face and his body language showed that he was:

        a. interested   b. bored   c. sick

New social situations can make us nervous. Experienced people will usually share social tips if they know we are _____.

1. For what reason did Alan's mom say an RSVP was needed?
2. Why is an RSVP a polite thing to do?
3. What might happen if the boys decided not to RSVP?
4. What are two tips that Alan's mom gave him for being social?

Doing the RSVP Thing | Page 185

Vocabulary

especially - *above all, particularly*
Maria especially wanted to be on time for her meeting with Shana.

obviously - *clearly seen, evidently*
Kim burst into the room, obviously very upset.

concerned - *worried, anxious*
Kim was very concerned that Bianca was missing.

employee - *worker, someone hired to do a job*
Bianca caused much anxiety as a missing employee.

novella

31 The Missing Employee
Making Good Choices

"That's what friends are for, isn't it?"

"Of course I'll do it. That's what friends are for, isn't it?" Maria told Bianca on the phone. She felt glad to be able to return a favor for Bianca's help with the spilled files.

Maria hurried to make it to work on time. The bus trip went smoothly. Sign-in took her a bit longer than usual and so did punching the time clock. With a bit of rushing, Maria was pleased that she still got to Shana's office before eight.

The Missing Employee | Page 187

"Bianca is nowhere to be found."

Shana was seated at her desk. She looked up with a welcoming smile when she saw Maria. "Hi, Maria. You will be pleased that we will be doing some more cafeteria work training! Today we will focus on how a new cafeteria employee gets started on the job. This will be your second lesson of training for your dream job," Shana said with a twinkle in her eyes.

Before Maria could respond and show her pleasure, Kim, Bianca's job coach, burst into the room. She was obviously upset. Kim said, "I need some help, Shana. I don't know what to do. One of my best workers, Bianca Ortega, is nowhere to be found. She has always been on time and at her work station."

"She signed in and her time card has been punched."

Shana, in her steady voice, responded, "Calm down, Kim. Let's think this through before you panic. Perhaps she is out sick. Did you check the sign-in sheet and her time card?"

"I sure did. That's what I did first. She signed in and her time card has been punched. Then I checked the cafeteria, the ladies' room and the employees' locker room. She was not there. I am so concerned. What could have happened to her?" Kim asked.

"Yes, I can see you are upset," Shana replied. "Especially since Bianca has a good attendance record."

The Missing Employee | Page 189

"I signed her in and punched her time card."

Maria felt her stomach turn flips. Her hands got sweaty. She was scared to speak up. She had the answer to the mystery of the missing Bianca. Would Bianca be in trouble if she told? Would she be in trouble? She knew that she had to say something.

In a very quiet voice, Maria said, "I know what happened to Bianca. She called me this morning because she had gotten up too late to make it to work on time. We agreed that I would sign her in and punch her time card. She's okay. She just has not gotten here yet. Are we in trouble?"

Page 190 | Chapter 31

Questions:

Kim reported that Bianca was missing and asked for help. The look on Kim's face and her body language showed that she was very:

        a. happy   b. upset   c. tired

Supervising employees is a big responsibility. When something happens to someone for whom we are responsible, we feel _____ .

    1. What did Maria agree to do for her friend, Bianca?

    2. Why was Kim, Bianca's job coach, so upset?

    3. Why didn't Maria immediately tell why Bianca was missing?

    4. In what way could Maria's actions have affected the work situation?

Vocabulary

blame - *fault, guilt*
Shana did not blame Maria entirely for the problem.

trust - *faith, belief*
Trust develops when people demonstrate honest and caring behavior.

fragile - *easily broken*
Trust is fragile.

respect - *value, high opinion*
In a real friendship, people show respect for one another.

agreement - *contract*
Employers and employees have an agreement or a two-way relationship.

dishonest - *lying, untruthful*
Maria said she did not mean to be dishonest.

opportunity - *chance*
An employer provides an employee with the opportunity to work and earn money.

demonstrate - *to show*
An employee can demonstrate respect for an employer by doing a good job.

novella

32 Broken Trust
Responsibility to an Employer

"Can you explain why you decided to sign Bianca in?"

Maria's progress at work seemed like a roller coaster ride. Some days she did really well. Other days weren't so great. Today was one of those other days. She felt very low. She had really messed up. Then, she remembered that Shana had told her that we learn important lessons from our mistakes.

Shana had arranged for Maria to remain in her office for a conference. Maria felt upset and a bit frightened at the serious look on Shana's face. Shana said, "Can you explain why you decided to sign Bianca in?"

Broken Trust | Page 193

"I wanted to be a good friend."

With an unsteady voice, Maria answered, "I wanted to be a good friend to Bianca. She had helped me when I really needed a friend to help. It seemed so easy and I didn't think it would hurt anyone."

"Maria, I'm all in favor of you being a good friend, but in this case I think that you made a very poor choice of how to do it. But, I realize that I cannot blame you entirely. I should have talked to you about the meaning of trust when you started working here. Trust is fragile. It develops when people demonstrate honest and caring behavior. In a real friendship, people show respect for each other and for themselves. Lying or not living up to agreements breaks trust."

"I did not mean to be dishonest. I didn't think…"

"But I didn't lie. Bianca asked me to sign her in and punch her time card. I did exactly what I told Bianca I would do," Maria protested.

"True," Shana went on, "but I believe you made your decision too quickly. There was more to think about. Were you honest to yourself and to your employer? Pretending that Bianca was here meant that she would be paid for work she did not do. That is not honest."

"I did not mean to be dishonest. I didn't think…" Maria had trouble continuing. Tears began to roll down her face.

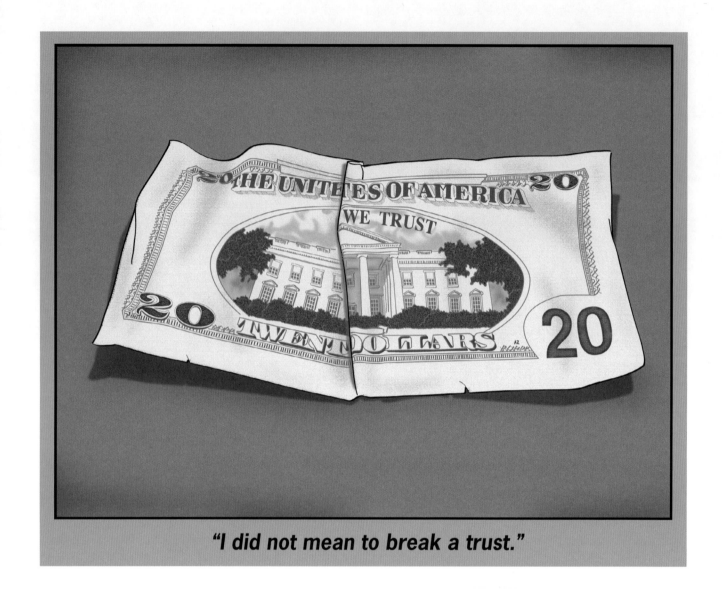

"I did not mean to break a trust."

"Yes, Maria. I think that the bottom line here involves not thinking your actions through. Not doing that caused problems. There is a two-way relationship between employer and employees. Your employer provides you with the opportunity to work and earn money. In return, the employee is expected to perform to the best of her ability and to demonstrate respect for her employer and her coworkers. Cheating or lying is disrespectful and damages trust."

"I really messed up, Shana. I'm so sorry. I did not mean to break a trust."

Questions:

Maria and Shana shook hands after a serious discussion about Maria's actions. Shaking hands after serious discussions can show that people:

  a. disagree about something   b. agree about something   c. are annoyed

Shaking hands during introductions shows respect and pleasure. Shaking hands after a discussion can mean that you both _____ .

    1. How was Maria's progress at work like a roller coaster?

    2. In what way was Maria dishonest?

    3. What did Shana explain to Maria about trust?

    4. How is honesty and trust important in a work setting?

Broken Trust | Page 197

Vocabulary

privately - *in secret or alone*
   Maria wished to talk to Bianca privately.

silence - *quiet*
   Both of the girls sat in silence waiting for the other to talk.

annoyance - *feeling of impatience or mild anger*
   Maria felt annoyance with Bianca's answer.

dishonest - *lying, untruthful*
   Did you think that you were asking me to be dishonest?

novella

33 Lighten Up
Responding to a Complaint

"When will this day ever end?"

The rest of the day dragged on for Maria. She was very upset with herself. She had made a poor choice that caused many problems. This was one workday she wished would end. Why hadn't she thought things through? Why had she put Bianca's request ahead of being honest? She was torn between wanting to see Bianca and wanting to avoid Bianca altogether. Maria's stomach was still churning. She thought, "When will this day ever end?"

Lighten Up | Page 199

Tears ran down Bianca's face.

As Maria was thinking over what had happened, she noticed Bianca come out of Kim's office. Tears were running down Bianca's face. Her eyes were red. Bianca hurried to her workstation without her usual smile and jokes. Maria decided they had to talk but certainly not now. Since tomorrow was a holiday, they would have plenty of time to discuss privately what they had done.

The next day, the girls were quieter than usual. Both looked as if they hoped the other would begin the conversation. It was Maria who broke the silence. "Bianca, did you think about being dishonest when you asked me to sign you in?"

"Hey, what difference did it make if I was a little late?"

Bianca responded immediately, "No. Hey, what difference did it make if I was a little late? I figured I'd get to work before anyone noticed."

"Well, it sure didn't work out that way. Did you think that you were asking me to be dishonest? Did you consider that I might get in trouble?" Maria asked with annoyance.

"Nope. I figured that it was no big deal. You are my friend. I help you. You help me. Lighten up, Maria. It's all over," Bianca replied as if she hadn't a care in the world.

Lighten Up | Page 201

"I can't just forget about it."

Maria felt annoyed but continued, "It looks like I have to learn everything the hard way. I don't want to lie, not for anyone, not even for my best friend. Maybe this is another lesson learned from a mistake."

"What's done is done. Forget about it," Bianca answered. She did not seem the least bit upset.

"I can't just forget about it. I wish I hadn't done it. I think it will take a while for Shana to trust me again. Also, I love my job. I don't want to be fired. I want to be a responsible worker, not a cheat," Maria responded seriously.

Questions:

The girls did not feel the same way about Maria signing Bianca in. Maria's face showed that she was:

      a. happy   b. upset   c. tired

When we do something without considering the consequences, afterward we may be _____ and wonder why we did it.

1. When did Maria plan to talk to Bianca about what they had done?
2. How did Maria and Bianca react differently to the situation?
3. What reasons did Maria give for being upset?
4. Which of the girls do you think will make a better employee? Why?

Lighten Up | Page 203

Vocabulary

admitted - *accepted as true*
Maria admitted to her mother that she felt confused.

trustworthy - *honest, reliable*
Keep trying and you will become a trustworthy employee.

selfish - *self-centered*
Is it selfish to sometimes say no to a friend?

generous - *big-hearted, giving*
Good friends are kind and generous.

novella

34 Keep Trying
Becoming a Trustworthy Employee

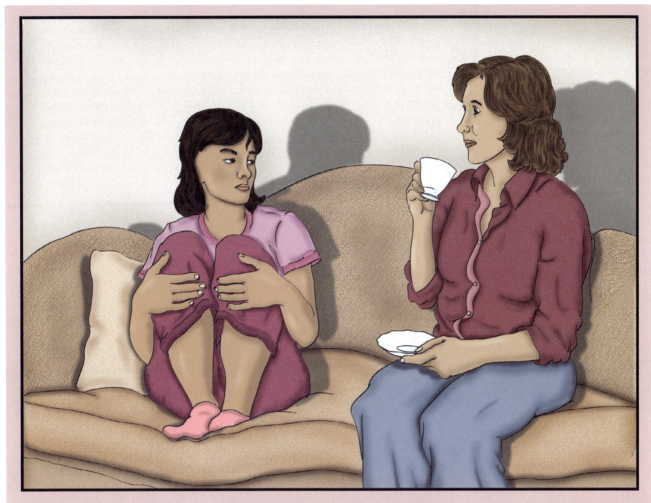

"Mom, I'm so confused."

Maria and her mom often sat in the living room after dinner. They chatted about the day while her mom enjoyed a cup of tea.

"Mom, I'm so confused about that mess Bianca and I got into," Maria admitted to her mother. "Can we talk about it? I feel terrible about it. Bianca just blew it off. She says it was nothing. How can we feel so differently?"

Keep Trying | Page 205

"How do I know what is more important?"

Mom took a sip of tea and then responded, "Friends often see and do things differently. What you both did involved more than yourselves. You girls did not consider the larger picture. Your behaviors involved your work, your job coaches and your employer. Also, many employees could have been affected by your actions."

"Oh, Mom, I have so many questions," Maria continued. "How do I know what is more important? Should I think of my friends first? What about my employer? And how about me? Am I selfish if I say no to a best friend?"

"Think of a STOP sign."

This time mom replied with a serious tone, "Saying no to a friend because you feel something is wrong or dishonest can be kind and generous. Always, you must try to be true to yourself. If something you are thinking about doing or saying makes you feel uncomfortable, STOP. Think of a STOP sign. Don't do or say anything until you think through what might happen if you do. Lying and cheating are traps that can lead to more dishonest behavior."

"I am really mixed up! I don't get it. How can saying no to a friend be kind and generous?" Maria asked.

"Just keep trying, Maria…"

"Real friends look out for each other. If you had pretended that you were not bothered by what you both had done, Bianca would have thought that lying and cheating were okay with you. Also, you both work for and accept a paycheck from an employer. Good workers are trustworthy. I know you will learn from this lesson. Just keep trying, Maria, and you'll become a fine, trustworthy employee."

"Mom, does this mean that Bianca won't be my best friend anymore?"

"I can't answer that for you, Maria. Only you can decide what you expect from a best friend."

Questions:

Maria and her mom discussed the situation. Her mother's face showed that she was listening and was very:

        a. concerned   b. angry   c. excited

It can be helpful to turn to a trustworthy adult with a problem. A parent, job coach or good friend will listen carefully to show that they are _____.

1. Why did Maria feel confused?
2. What did Maria's mom tell Maria about being true to herself?
3. Describe how the two friends seemed to view 'the mess'.
4. Describe Bianca's behavior as a best friend, coworker and employee.

Vocabulary

host - *person caring for guests*
It is polite to show respect for the host of the party.

casual - *relaxed, not formal*
Sandals, shorts and a tee shirt may be acceptable at a casual party.

guests - *visitors, company*
Polite people respect the host and other guests attending the party.

appearance - *way something looks*
Your neat and clean appearance is one way to show respect for yourself and others.

confident - *sure of abilities*
Jerome did not feel confident picking out clothes for Shana's party.

novella
35 Getting Ready
Clothes and Social Behavior

He didn't know anything about girls.

Jerome worked hard all week but no matter what he was doing, his thoughts kept returning to Friday night's party. He wanted to see his friends from the training center. Alan told him that some girls were going. That scared Jerome. He didn't know anything about girls, except Ellie and Shana. And, of course his mom and his aunts. But they didn't count as girls. Jerome had two brothers. He was sure that was why he could talk to 'guys' better than girls.

Getting Ready | Page 211

"Hey, Nat, how do you decide what to wear?"

Jerome's older brother, Nat, was comfortable around girls. Jerome decided to ask him for help. Mom had given him the perfect chance. She had turned over the cooking responsibilities to the two brothers for the evening. Jerome and Nat were out in the yard talking while they cooked dinner on the grill.

"Hey, Nat, how do you decide what to wear when you go out?" Jerome asked.

"Well, Jerome, first I think about where I'll be going. That helps me make a decision. Let me ask you. Would you wear a bathing suit to the movies? Would you wear your dress jacket to the beach?"

"Don't be silly, of course not," Jerome responded shaking his head.

Page 212 | Chapter 35

"I like to be comfortable."

Nat grinned as he said, "I wasn't trying to be silly. Thinking about where you are going will help you decide what to wear. What would you feel comfortable wearing for Shana's party?"

"I like my camouflage shorts and tee shirt and my sandals," Jerome quickly answered. "They are comfortable. I like to be comfortable."

"True, they would be comfortable. But comfort isn't everything when you are invited to a party. You are expected to show respect for the host and all the guests. Your appearance and your choice of clothes help do that."

"Usually long pants are more acceptable."

Nat continued, "Usually long pants and a polo shirt or a shirt that buttons are more acceptable, as well as some kind of shoes that cover your feet. That's what I have found to be appropriate, unless the invitation says 'casual'. Did your invitation say that?" Nat asked.

"No! Oh, boy, now what? Will you help me pick out an outfit? I don't feel confident that I can pick out something that will be right. I bet you know what girls like. I don't want to look funny, especially if girls are there!"

Questions:

Jerome turned to his older brother, Nat, for help. Nat's body language and facial expressions showed:

        a. anger   b. interest   c. sadness

Family members often help each other by listening and sharing experiences about social situations. This behavior shows _____ .

1. Why was Jerome nervous about talking to girls?
2. What person did Jerome ask for help and why?
3. What might have happened if Jerome had worn his camouflage shorts, tee shirt and sandals to Shana's party?
4. How can a choice of clothing show respect for the host and guests?

Getting Ready | Page 215